AFTER
McDONALDIZATION

Also by John Drane

Do Christians Know How to Be Spiritual?
The McDonaldization of the Church

Family Fortunes
(with Olive M. Fleming Drane)

AFTER
McDONALDIZATION

Mission, Ministry, and Christian Discipleship in an Age of Uncertainty

JOHN DRANE

Baker Academic
a division of Baker Publishing Group
www.BakerAcademic.com

© 2008 by John Drane

Published in the United States by Baker Academic
a division of Baker Publishing Group
P.O. Box 6287, Grand Rapids, MI 49516-6287
www.bakeracademic.com

First published by Darton, Longman and Todd Ltd., London, UK

Typeset by YHT Ltd, London
Printed and bound in Great Britain by
CPI Antony Rowe, Chippenham

Library of Congress Cataloging-in-Publication Data is on file
at the Library of Congress in Washington, DC

ISBN 978–0-8010–3611–8

CONTENTS

Preface   vii

1. Culture   1

2. Community   29

3. Mission   59

4. Ministry   93

5. Theology   118

   Notes   143

   Bibliography   155

   Index   161

PREFACE

This book has been in the pipeline ever since the publication of its predecessor, *The McDonaldization of the Church*, in 2000,[1] for I always knew that if we were to move on from the limitations of a McDonaldized way of being church, it would be important to give some thought to what might come next. As it happened, what came next was a massive shift in cultural attitudes right across the world following the events of what we have come to call simply '9/11', and the fear and uncertainty that created has had a significant impact on people's attitudes to religion of all sorts, Christianity included. At the same time, many churches are now facing up to the reality of the decline that has been affecting all major denominations for 20 years and more, and are realizing that to continue as we are may be comfortable, but could also be institutionally suicidal. Our options are simple. We either do nothing, and the decline continues, or we ask fundamental questions about how faithful discipleship might be incarnationally embedded in the culture, and take whatever steps may be necessary to re-imagine church life. This second option can look threatening, but the worst possible scenario that could come of it would be that we fail in the enterprise of radically re-imagining church, which if it happened would leave us in exactly the same position as if we do nothing. On the other hand, if we truly believe in a God whose primary attribute is creativity and imagination (Gen. 1:1—2:4a) – not to mention one who moves mountains – then we can step out in faith into even risky spaces, confident in the knowledge that we are not alone, and that God may well already be ahead of us.

Considering that this is a sequel to *The McDonaldization of the Church*, it should surprise no one that the book itself bears few signs of a McDonaldized argument. It is less of a neatly ordered discussion and more of an invitation to think outside the box of what we now know, and to imagine what the Christian future might look and feel like if we allow ourselves to ask new questions. Though each chapter has a different title, they are all interconnected, and what is said on one subject could just as easily have been said on another, to such an extent that much of the material is interchangeable. What is said on mission is relevant to the chapter on ministry, while both are relevant to the discussions of community, culture, and theology. Daniel Pink (one-time speech-writer for US vice-president Al Gore) suggests that the skills we ought to be fostering in order to cope with the rapidly changing cultural context of today's world consist of:

> the ability to put together the pieces ... to synthesize rather than to analyze; to see relationships between seemingly unrelated fields; to detect broad patterns rather than to deliver specific answers; and to invent something new by combining elements nobody else thought to pair.[2]

I am trying to do something like that here. Those who think in this sort of cyclical way will love it, while readers who prefer a more linear form of argument that has a beginning, a middle and an ending will find it more challenging, and quite probably a fair number will dismiss it out of hand for that reason.

Another aspect of this book that is worth commenting on is the fact that I have deliberately included a fair number of personal stories. There is a reason for this that goes well beyond mere self-indulgence. For story is central to the Gospel, and story reaches places and refreshes parts that abstract reasoning can never touch. Cognitive analysis may be highly valued in the rarefied atmosphere of the academy, but story is the stuff of life, inviting us to reflect on our own lives even as we learn from the experiences of others. Academics claim to be objective and detached, but the very methods that are supposed to deliver this detachment can also serve as a convenient way of not facing up to reality. To be human is to have a story, indeed to be a story. By sharing stories we hold a mirror up to ourselves, something that in turn encourages deeper reflection. If we are to engage other people's stories, we must first be honest about our own – but also be aware of how all our individual stories relate to that over-arching narrative that is God's story.

One advantage of having taken so long to complete this project is that everything in here has been shared with church leaders from many different theological and ecclesiastical traditions, and in numerous countries, not just in seminars and clergy retreats but also at local parish level. For that reason, I am confident that what is said here not only resonates with the questions that so many Christians now have, but also suggests ways of addressing them that are transferable across a whole range of environments, church styles, and individual personality types.

I have learned a good deal from discussing these matters with others, and two deserve special mention. In 2006, my wife Olive and I led a clergy retreat for the Diocese of St Asaph of the (Anglican) Church in Wales, and in thanking us at the end of the day the bishop, the Rt Revd John Davies, offered the opinion that today's people 'seem to be more afraid of living than they are of dying'. The immediate context in which he said it was a session that Olive had led on the subject of her own book, *Spirituality to Go*, which offers 'rituals and reflections for everyday living'.[3] I have no idea if Bishop John even remembers using that phrase, but I immediately recognized that it was going to be important in relation to the mission of the Church. Without his comment, much of what is said here about mission and spirituality would have been very differently expressed. The others I must mention are members of the Mission Theological Advisory Group, which for the last five years I have co-chaired along with the Rt Revd David Atkinson, Bishop of Thetford.[4] That period included a very painful episode which led to my resigning from what I had assumed would be a job for life, and changed the whole course of the rest of my life and ministry. My colleagues on that group not only prayed for me and with me, but throughout our discussions about the state of the churches and the prospects for missional engagement with the culture, I found them to be theological and ecclesiastical soul-mates who both inspired and supported one another in a way that is far from typical of a church committee, but which reinforced for me the importance of living the Gospel and not just talking about it.

Of course, none of these people are responsible for what is in here. It certainly will not be the last word on these important subjects – not even my own last word! One other thing I have learned in this process is the importance of not taking ourselves too seriously. I therefore invite readers to engage with it all in the spirit of the comedian Groucho Marx, who famously said, 'These are my opinions – if you don't like them, I can always offer you some others.'

JOHN DRANE
Feast of St James the Apostle, 2007

1 CULTURE

A personal perspective

According to Michael Frost and Alan Hirsch, my previous book, *The McDonaldization of the Church*, 'created quite a stir' and is 'must-read material'.[1] More recently, it featured on a list as one of the six most influential books on emerging church.[2] It is of course every author's dream that others will respond to their work in that way, which no doubt has something to do with my reasons for referring to them here. They were not the only ones, though. Sociologist George Ritzer, who first coined the term 'McDonaldization' to describe a certain form of over-rationalized life, was another scholar who warmed to my work and soon included extracts from it in his widely read *McDonaldization Reader*,[3] and when the two of us presented a seminar together at Fuller Seminary in Pasadena, California, hundreds of people turned up to eavesdrop on our conversations. In the earlier part of my life, Christians generally connected me with the Bible, because they had come across my name through books on the Old and New Testaments that still remain exceedingly popular in the reading lists of theological colleges and seminaries right across the world.[4] But for the twenty-first century, I have had to live with the label of McDonaldization – to such an extent that when I visited as guest preacher a church where I had previously been a member, and then preached a sermon based on the lectionary reading for the day, the senior minister expressed some surprise that I was still interested in Scripture, and even more taken aback that I was seeking to integrate it with what he regarded as my new-found fascination with the social sciences. His perception of my spiritual pilgrimage was not quite accurate, however, as my interest in the Bible had always been driven by a concern for its contemporary relevance, even as long ago as when I was a student, as I shall explain in more detail in Chapter 5. Conversely, my understanding of the cultural challenges facing the Church had always been filtered through the insights of Scripture and the wider Christian tradition. There is no doubt, however, that my engagement with what I identified as the McDonaldization of the Church has had a more far-reaching impact on my life than ever I anticipated, and has opened up many opportunities for innovative ministry that might otherwise have passed me by. That was not the first book I had written on the theme of church and culture,[5] but it turned out to be the right book at the right time. Though the start of the new millennium was not marked by any of the apocalyptic crises that had been predicted by the doom-mongers, the two-or-three-year time-frame that covered the end of the twentieth century and the start of the twenty-first did offer an opportunity for us all to reflect on where we have come from, who we now are, and where we might go in the future. I was not consciously thinking of it in those terms at the time, but with hindsight I think that writing *The McDonaldization of the Church* filled that role for me, offering a sort of mid-life assessment of the Church as I had experienced it, and my hopes and aspirations for the future.

By then, I had been actively involved in church life for many years, initially in local contexts, but then from the mid 1980s and throughout the 1990s I found myself thrust into the role of a leader in national and international events. For much of that period I had both chaired and been a member of a number of significant ecumenical committees in the UK. It was a time of rapid change, as ways of being that had served our forebears well for centuries were questioned and, in many cases, discarded. What was taking place in the wider culture was bound to impinge on the life of the Church, though it was some time before church leaders woke up to that reality and started to engage with its implications. But those with the vision to see it understood that structures and procedures that had apparently stood the test of time would no longer work in the new emerging cultural environment – indeed, that the whole fabric of faith was being stretched and tested in a way that was well beyond the previous experience of any of us. The idea that Christian faith might be challenged, and the Church discredited, was nothing new. From its inception, the Church faced enemies who wanted to destroy it. But in the more recent past the attempts to undermine the Church's credibility had tended to be mostly of an intellectual nature, focusing on things like the historical reliability of the Bible or arguments about science and religion. Though there was by no means one single opinion on an appropriately Christian response to such questions, church leaders knew how to engage with these and similar topics, because traditional theological education had embraced them, often to such an extent that newly qualified graduates complained with some justice that they knew more about academic opinions on the Bible than they did about the actual text of Scripture itself. But by the end of the twentieth century, the notion of foundational wisdom in the inherited philosophical sense was no longer regarded as the touchstone of what might be meaningful and true. That meant the ground was shifting in upheavals of seismic proportions, as the rules of the game were rewritten to accommodate new ways of seeing things. Rational engagement with what had been regarded as objective truth was replaced by relevance as a key criterion by which the value of anything was now to be judged. Wrestling with increasingly pressurized lifestyles, and challenged by the near-meltdown of traditional institutional structures, not to mention a growing awareness of the need to live more harmoniously with the rest of the world, people in the Global North found themselves with neither the time nor the inclination for the religious pursuits of their forebears.[6] To be meaningful – and therefore worth pursuing – faith had to connect more obviously with the issues of lifestyle with which we now had to wrestle, and that meant it had to relate to this life here and now and not just to some esoteric notion of life in another world.

Faced with this new agenda (and what I have described here is only the tip of a very large cultural iceberg), the churches soon found themselves struggling, because the gap between the culture of the Church and the lived experience even of its members was expanding almost on a daily basis. Growing numbers of young people found little that spoke to them, and either left the Church or never connected with it in the first place. As will be suggested in later chapters, there are good reasons for supposing that their disillusionment was not directly connected with the Gospel as such, but rather they were unable to get beyond the institutional structures and systems in which the message had been embodied. Now, as we move toward the end of the first decade of the twenty-first century, an even more threatening trend has emerged, as middle-aged people find themselves growing weary of the ways of congregations to which they have belonged for much of their lives, and in many cases these are people who have hitherto been actively involved either as lay leaders or in full-time ministry.[7] Though this is not the whole picture, and there are also some more hopeful signs, the facts still make depressing reading. If nothing changes, then present statistical indicators suggest that the Church in Wales (Anglican) will be unsustainable by 2020, the United Reformed Church will disappear in 2022, the Church of Scotland by 2033, and the British Methodist Church will have zero membership by 2037.[8] By contrast, the situation is very different in the Global South, and some church leaders are inclined to believe that we can look there to reinvent the Church in other, once-Christian cultures. It would be foolish to imagine that we have nothing to learn from the phenomenal growth of the Christian community in places like Africa, China, parts of south-east Asia, and South America – and it is notable that in most parts of the Global North the only churches that are growing are those whose ministry is predominantly among immigrant populations from these other parts of the world. But the reasons for the growth of such churches are very varied, and not all of them can easily be correlated with the current concerns of the majority population in the Global North. Spiritual desires are not the only component, and in many parts of the world other factors such as increased literacy, the birth rate, and globalization are all playing a part in the growth of the Church, and in some cases may be more significant than religious faith in and of itself. The rapid movement of people driven by war and economic migration has brought non-traditional forms of Christian devotion into many cities in Europe, North America, and Australasia. But the growth of such congregations will not make a significant difference to the overall fate of the Church in these places. Wherever we look, it is the same scenario, albeit with regional variations.

The contours of the landscape are different in the USA, where church membership can still call forth some degree of civic approval (and where the diversity of Christian denominations has always been far greater than in Europe), though even there the future is much less secure than it looks from the outside, especially among the mainline denominations. Regular attendance at American churches has conventionally been placed at around 60 per cent of the population, but the outlook is far less certain than that sort of statistic might suggest. There are various reasons for this. One factor that is more important than it might seem is the way that church attendance in the USA has traditionally been counted, through opinion polls rather than by the use of hard statistical evidence. In the sort of religiously observant culture that the USA still is, when people are asked if they have been to church on the previous Sunday, they are more likely to say yes than no, which inevitably tends to distort the real picture. In those cases where more exact measurements of church membership and attendance have been gathered, the American figure turns out to be nearer 20 per cent than 60 per cent, though with enormous variations from one state to another. Research conducted early in 2007 showed that roughly 100 million Americans, or about 34 per cent of the population, have no connection with any church at all.[9] That is still way better than the figures for any other country in the Global North (including neighbouring Canada), but it hardly means that American churches can rest on their laurels. By definition, a free market enterprise culture does not encourage even short-term loyalty, and recent research has documented the growing popularity of new forms of faith activity among American Christians (things like home churches, marketplace ministries, and cyberchurch), with one commentator predicting that even those who are committed to regular prayer, Bible reading and spiritual direction will in future be doing so without any formal connection with congregational life.[10] Moreover, the diversity is not limited to pragmatic considerations, but extends to significant, and maybe incompatible, understandings of the nature of God and God's relationship to the world and its people.[11]

In reflecting on the reasons for all this, there is only one absolutely indisputable fact, and that is that there is no single or simple explanation that can be given. Such serious decline in an institution that has defined the Western world since the days of the Roman emperor Constantine (AD 280–337) has not come about overnight, nor is it likely that, being in the midst of it as we are, any one of us now living will be able to discern all the details of the big cultural picture. There is no doubt that in the second half of the twentieth century the processes identified as McDonaldization played a significant part, as people who felt oppressed by the over-rationalization of the workplace sought a space of renewal, only to find that the churches offered the same sort of homogenized and rigidly structured culture that they were trying to escape, and as a consequence many headed off in the direction of so-called 'alternative' spiritualities and therapies in the search for personal wholeness.[12] It is impossible to exaggerate the part played in Church decline by the loss of confidence in the Church among those who are self-consciously searching for spiritual meaning and purpose in life.

I have argued elsewhere that, though the categories of McDonaldization offer us an exceedingly useful tool for understanding the predicament in which the Church now finds itself, the attitudes and mindsets that underpin such over-rationalized ways of being are not actually a twentieth-century invention, but can be traced in embryonic form back through the history of Christendom and ultimately to the Roman empire.[13] If there is any truth in that claim, then we have to admit that a McDonaldized form of church seems to have been pretty successful (at least in terms of numbers and influence) for a very long time. To use missiological jargon, that form of church was clearly well contextualized in a highly rationalized society – though whether it was also an authentic contextualization of the Gospel is now widely regarded as a matter of opinion. Making such value judgements on the past is always easy with the benefit of hindsight, but whatever we think of our Christian forebears, there can be no question that one of the reasons why the Church has hit upon hard times now is because the culture has changed in such a way that we are less tolerant of rationalized structures, at least in those areas of life where we can exercise our own free choice. At the same time, we have a cultural ambivalence about all this, and we both love and hate McDonaldization. We deplore it in terms of our inner and private personal lives while at the same time accepting it as an unavoidable everyday reality in the workplace and in civic life. Even there, though, there is a widespread recognition that we should be trying to give a more human face to the structures created by McDonaldized thinking, but paradoxically we generally tackle even that through the development of yet more rationalized systems! However, in those aspects of life where we do not need to be submissive to such restrictions, we tend to make different choices – and that includes church (indeed, religious belief more widely), for reasons that are again not hard to identify. There is much to be said in favour of the Reformation insistence that Christian belief is essentially a personal matter between an individual and God, but equally there can be no doubt that (notwithstanding the efforts of Calvin and others to encourage a corporate dimension to faith) what is personal has easily transformed itself into something private in a way that, in a consumerist culture, means it is relegated to a leisure activity for those who happen to be interested in such things. Not only has this led to a marginalization of faith as being the concern only of a particular interest group, but it has also helped to create an environment in which people find themselves both mystified and threatened by other religious traditions that take it for granted that faith ought to be a holistic matter that infuses and informs every aspect of life. One of the ironies of current political moves to create an inclusive society in which all faiths can flourish is that the underlying secular agenda of the political chattering classes assumes that all cultures are provisional and relative, and therefore equally unimportant and meaningless. It is an easy matter to appear to accept everything if it is all relative and of no ultimate consequence, and it should surprise no one that the representatives of faiths such as Islam, which do still have a holistic view of life, should be suspicious of this sort of 'openness' as being just another example of a bankrupt Western culture seeking to colonize the rest of the world through the relativizing of all truth claims.[14]

The triumph of pragmatism

In recent years, Christians have expended an enormous amount of energy in the effort to engage with all this. The most common approach has been to try to understand the question from an intellectual, philosophical angle, by identifying and analyzing the worldview that has come to dominate in the Global North. Tackling the matter in this way itself raises some interesting questions about the Church and its predicament. It suggests that we believe that this culture actually has a coherent worldview comparable with the foundational certainties of the past; and it also implies that there is some underlying set of such principles that drive and inform the multifarious ways in which we now seek to live the good life. Neither of these assumptions can be accepted without more reflection. The average person in the street may not have been able to articulate it very precisely, but for generations our forebears took it for granted that there was an over-arching structure and rationality to life, all of it grounded in big ideas about ultimate reality and the ways in which that reality could be understood and reflected upon. The worldview of modernity was characterized by this sort of rational certainty, and its practical outcomes were made possible through scientific and technological progress. This way of looking at life is often characterized as the outcome of 'the Enlightenment', and it is regularly blamed for most of the cultural woes that we are wrestling with today. Even popular celebrities get in on the act. British TV chef Hugh Fearnley-Whittingstall's *River Cottage Meat Book* opens with a whole chapter on the philosophy of food, tracing what the author believes to be our unhealthy attitudes back to the influence of René Descartes (1596–1650) and his successors.[15] Christians are no different, and in the search for an instant scapegoat, have often been inclined to blame 'the Enlightenment' for all the Church's problems. Actually, the concept of 'the Enlightenment' is itself a problematic and contested category, and at the very least it is not as self-contained as the use of that single word implies. In many ways, it was simply an outworking of concepts that had been there all along in ancient Greek philosophy and Roman pragmatism. But by apportioning all the blame to that intellectual movement which swept through Europe in the seventeenth and eighteenth centuries, we have also shielded ourselves from the uncomfortable possibility that the values represented by that terminology might actually be deeply rooted within the historic Christian tradition itself.

This is not the place to take a detour into the Enlightenment and its history. However we perceive it, the highly differentiated social structure that it produced is still familiar to most of us, if only by hearsay from previous generations of our own families. Its quintessential heyday, at least in a British context, was the Victorian and Edwardian eras (roughly the mid nineteenth century to the time of World War I), when everyone and everything (including God and the Church) had a place, and everyone knew what their place was. Today, that kind of society has gone. When I first wrote that last sentence, I put the word 'forever' at the end of it. But nothing lasts forever, and history has a habit of repeating itself. It is at least possible that Western people, faced with a culture that is becoming ever more meaningless almost on a daily basis, and struggling with the personal anxieties which that induces, may yet choose to revert to a worldview of certainties in the form of some kind of spiritual pathway that makes strident lifestyle demands on its followers.

As things are today, however, I am not at all convinced that most people in the Global North have any sort of coherent worldview, and the lack of any meaningful frame of reference within which to understand ourselves or the world is one of the biggest challenges we face if our civilization is not to implode on itself. The popular pundits, of course, insist that we are now living in a 'post-modern' world. Christians, even more than others, seem to have caught onto this way of speaking – as if having the right words with which to describe the culture will somehow ensure that we know how to live effectively within it. But just attaching a label to it does not by itself offer a sufficient explanation of what is going on. In any case, the terminology itself is ambiguous, and quite apart from discussions about the reality that it may be intended to signify, a baffling array of different words are currently in vogue: postmodernism (or post-modernism), postmodernity (also sometimes with a hyphen), post-Christian, secular, post-secular, late modernity, liquid modernity, post-Christendom, and many others. Those who use these terms do not always define them carefully, and in some cases I suspect that people use them without having much idea of what they mean. This evident lack of clarity is one reason why we ought to regard these nostrums with a degree of scepticism. The more likely reality is that we have no idea what is going on in the culture. At the same time, having a single word can be helpful, just so long as we realize that any term we adopt is going to be at best provisional, and quite possibly misleading or inaccurate. For simplicity's sake, I still use this language, though my preference is to speak of post-modernity, with a hyphen, which is intended to indicate that this is not a precise definition – still less a 'worldview' – but rather is a shorthand way of referring to the chaos into which things descended once the previous worldview of modernity began to be questioned and rejected. Martyn Percy grasps the reality of this when he observes that whatever post-modernity is, it is 'not a systematic philosophical system; it is more of a mood and a socio-cultural force'.[16] Future generations will be better placed than us to discern whether post-modernity turns out to be anything more substantial than that, though on the basis of all the available evidence right now, it strikes me as unlikely that either 'post-modernity' or any of the other terms in common use represent any sort of coherent worldview in the sense with which past generations would have used the word. I suspect that our concern about terminology at this point is a smo-kescreen that enables us to conceal our much deeper fear of what is unknown. By putting a label on whatever is going on, we can con-vince ourselves that we know what it is, and behind that is the thought that if we are able to name it correctly, we might also be able to control it. Unfortunately this is just wishful thinking, and Western culture is in a much bigger mess than most of us would like to acknowledge.

That is not to say that today's people are (to use a traditional word) irrational. But both the source and the nature of today's rationality are different from those of previous generations. One reason why it is so difficult to get a handle on the deeply held values of contemporary Western culture is that the way in which culture is formed has itself undergone a radical change, even since the start of the twenty-first century. For a thousand years and more, cultural norms in a hierarchical society were established by the agenda that was set by philosophers, politicians, and generals (who were often the same people), and everyone else simply accepted their ideas. If ordinary people held different opinions, they had no significant forum in which to express them. The rise of democracy was an attempt to address this, by giving everyone a voice, but even here the agenda was limited to whatever was on offer from the intellectual and political establishment of the day, because democratic choice never offers complete freedom but only the opportunity to choose between whatever alternatives are made available. Over the last 40 years or so, there has been a gradual shift of awareness in relation to the nature of personal freedom, but the development of the internet and the worldwide web has, within the last decade, quite literally given a voice to everyone with access to a computer. Not only have blog sites, bulletin boards, and other forms of digital dialogue given a voice to those who would otherwise never be heard, but the entire phenomenon has become a channel for subverting the existing systems. It can be argued that this has merely created a different sort of élite, depending now not on accidents of birth, inheritance, or education, but on ownership of or access to a computer and the internet. Whether or not that is true, it is certainly the case that these new media have given a platform to a greater number of ordinary people than ever before, and opinions on significant lifestyle issues are no longer handed down from those who are supposed to know, but are more likely to be aired first among ordinary people, and then politicians and others begin to take notice. This new reality does not prevent some academics from continuing to behave as if they were still the trend-setters, but that attitude can now only be sustained by a resolutely head-in-the-sand approach that deliberately disconnects itself from the feelings and opinions of the wider population.[17]

In relation to the Church's future, then, it seems to me that the reality with which we should be engaging is more about lifestyles and personal perspectives than about anything we might call a 'worldview'. Or, let me express it in a different way that redefines 'worldview': what if our everyday life and experience actually *is* our worldview? What happens if we prioritize experience over and above reason? The traditional answer offered by a modernist mindset would be that we are on a slippery slope indeed, because the authenticity of experience could never be taken for granted but was always to be tested by reference to the canons of rationality.

That is actually an unnecessary dichotomy, especially in a Christian frame of reference, because both experience and rationality are intrinsic parts of the human psyche, which is itself 'made in the image of God' (Gen. 1:27). In any case, few people are all experience and no reason. A more common way of processing life's reality is to reflect on the meaning of what happens, asking questions about the way in which disparate experiences connect together, if indeed they do. Though that process transgresses the philosophical norms of the past, I suspect that most people have always understood life in this way, and the only reason we fail to recognize it is because those voices from the past that we know about are not the voices of ordinary individuals, but of élites of various kinds.[18] We will return in a later chapter to this theme of how we process reality, because it seems to me to be of considerable importance in relation to understanding how we might be appropriately Christian in today's world. For now, though, we can use it to explore the question of what is going on in the culture.

New experiences, new questions

Until relatively recently, cultural analysts have generally eschewed popular (or folk) culture as a way of truly understanding what is going on in society.[19] But if we emphasize the primacy of high culture (by which I mean the preferences of the intellectual chattering classes), we are likely to miss some of the most significant movements of our time – especially when viewed from a Christian perspective, which ought to prioritize what is personal and relational over and above what is abstract and analytical. Approaching the subject from this angle, we can identify four significant experiences that people have to deal with in everyday life, that are formative in relation to personal attitudes, and which Christians ought therefore to be taking seriously. First of all is the fact that everyday life presents us with the realization that *nothing seems to work the way it once did*. I am reminded of this every morning when I get out of bed and make breakfast, because the experience is totally different from anything that my own grandparents could have imagined (or, for that matter, my parents in their earlier years). I rise in a room that, no matter what the season or the outside temperature, is likely to be at a comfortable temperature, whereas my grandparents never had any sort of air-conditioning system (whether heating or cooling) in their entire lives, and (living, as they did, in a generally cold climate) could only have imagined what a warm house might feel like. Beyond that, if they were to come into my kitchen today, they might as well be on another planet, because I doubt that they would know how to carry out any of the simple operations involved in something as straightforward as making breakfast. The food itself has changed remarkably little, but the way it is now prepared might require the use of a microwave oven – and even something as simple as getting water at the kitchen sink works in a different way than in my grandparents' home: they had functional taps with a knob to be turned, whereas mine has a fancy faucet with a handle to lift. The idea that I might watch breakfast TV, and that the electric kettle will turn itself off as it boils, or that a machine would make the coffee while I take a shower, would likewise be beyond anything they could have imagined – while the idea that I might simultaneously be exchanging email messages with friends or receiving on a cell-phone pictures of what others are doing on the other side of the world would only ever have been in the realms of unimaginable science fiction. The same would be true of almost any household activity, including cleaning and laundry. However, we do not need to go back a couple of generations to appreciate this. I got my first computer in the early 1990s, and it seemed like a miracle at the time. But by comparison with today's machines it was huge, slow, and difficult to use, because even a word-processing program required the memorization of countless keystrokes in order to make anything happen. Its entire capacity was less than one per cent of what I now have on a memory card that is the same size as a small postage stamp.

In a world of such rapid change, in which the pace of change itself is speeding up all the time, it is not only transient operations such as heating, cooking, or computing that no longer work according to old paradigms. Life itself – the way we live it as well as the way we understand it – has changed, and continues to do so. If a computer that was state-of-the-art 15 years ago is now a museum piece, how can we expect anything else to be long lasting? In particular, why should anyone imagine that the answers of our grandparents' generation to the most profound questions about the meaning of life should still make sense today, when our questions are so different? In most cultures of the Global South the wisdom of older people is still generally valued, but in a society where relationships themselves are increasingly fragmented, we are less likely to embrace the truth that inspired even our own immediate forebears. In this context, the Church is perceived as just one more thing that – whatever its usefulness to previous generations – is now well and truly past its sell-by date, 'something between a hobby with too many rules and a totalitarian regime'.[20] The Anglican researcher George Lings is not being cynical, but merely telling it how it is, when he writes that for many people,

> Church is what some others do. It is noticed sadly, in their terms, not only as an alien and expensive building that I wouldn't know what to do in, worse, it is occupied by people I wouldn't be seen dead with.[21]

A second significant experience for people today is the growing realization that *the way Western people have lived is not the only possible way to be*, nor is it the only one that looks as if it might lead to a fulfilled and meaningful life. A couple of generations ago, faiths other than Christianity were beyond the experience of most people in the Global North, whereas today they are on almost everyone's doorstep. But this is only one aspect of the diversity that we now experience in everyday life. Within the Christian Church itself, there is an awareness that there are many different ways of worshipping, and of doing theology. The rise of Pentecostalism, growing from literally nothing at the beginning of the twentieth century to be one of the major strands of the world Church today, is just one aspect of that.[22] And within the wider culture, the nature of leadership has changed, not only in the fact that women now share it with men, but in the realization that leadership itself need not be defined by reference to the sort of hierarchical models inherited from the past. All these factors have fed into the rise of New Spirituality, which is the term I now prefer for what would previously have been labelled 'New Age'. Traditional religions tend to be led by recognized authorities who exercise control over the beliefs and behaviour of their followers, and the same is generally true for New Religious Movements (by which I mean organizationally structured groups such as Scientology, the Unification Church, and so on).[23] But New Spirituality creates a space for us all to explore our own pathway, and assumes that – especially in spiritual matters – there can be no experts who know it all, only pilgrims who can share what they have learned in the course of their own journey through life.

The third notable feature of everyday post-modernity stems directly from that, in *the frequently expressed desire to be 'spiritual' rather than religious*. The reasons why this has come about are complex and contested,[24] but the phenomenon cannot be ignored in relation to what it might now mean to be Christian. An ethnographic study over an extended period of the spiritual and religious life of Kendal, a small town on the fringe of the English Lake District, demonstrated not only the reality of this shift, but also suggested that the rising interest in what the authors of that report called 'the holistic milieu' could be paralleled by a corresponding decline in adherence to the 'congregational domain' offered in the local churches.[25] Twenty years ago, Shirley Maclaine intuited the same conclusion, when she claimed that 'Your religions teach religion – not spirituality.'[26] It is certainly the case that, at the same time as the UK churches (of all denominations) have experienced significant decline, there has been a measurable growth in the popularity of new forms of experiential spirituality, whether that be through the study of the sort of arcane texts popularized by Dan Brown's novel, *The Da Vinci Code*,[27] or by experimenting with techniques to enhance spiritual awareness, or buying into so-called 'complementary' or 'alternative' healing therapies and so on. Moreover, a much publicized research project carried out by David Hay and Kate Hunt at the turn of the millennium revealed that such spiritual experience is apparently not restricted to those with an overt faith commitment, but is widespread within sections of the population that think of themselves as 'secular'.[28] George Ritzer succinctly expressed one of the reasons why we are so concerned to find that special experience which will make sense of life:

> Human beings, equipped with a wide array of skills and abilities, are asked to perform a limited number of highly simplified tasks over and over ... [are] forced to deny their humanity and act in a robot-like manner.[29]

When I first came across that statement, I realized that it could be applied as easily to church life as to any of the other rationalized systems with which we struggle in everyday life, which is why I then wrote a book about it. I will suggest in a later chapter that the Church is not really as 'unspiritual' as some people claim, and that the real problem is that we tend to operate with limited definitions of what 'spirituality' might entail. In the process of doing so, we too easily exclude whole areas of life that others would regard as the entry point for the spiritual search – hence the widely held perception among those people who ponder such things, that Christians are 'not spiritual'. There is a mission issue here, for surely those individuals who already believe that something 'spiritual' is important for a wholesome life are more likely to be interested in the Gospel than those who are avowed atheists or agnostics, which means that our ability to reach these people will play a key role in sustaining the Church of the future.[30]

A fourth characteristic of everyday life – and one that is growing in importance all the time – is *a consciousness that we live in fearful times*. Martin Rees is no scaremongering fundamentalist (he is the Astronomer Royal, and a professor at the University of Cambridge), but in his book *Our Final Century* he paints a bleak picture:

> I think the odds are no better than fifty-fifty that our present civilisation on Earth will survive to the end of the present century ... What happens here on Earth, in this century, could conceivably make the difference between a near eternity filled with ever more complex and subtle forms of life and one filled with nothing but base matter.[31]

The book makes depressing reading, as he lists all the possible ways in which the ultimate doomsday scenario might be played out, all of which are far more scary than they might otherwise seem, because they involve human error rather than deliberate actions on the part of either governments or criminals. Nevertheless, the presence of indiscriminate killers on the streets of cities around the world is reminding us of the fragility of human existence. Then even beyond issues of personal safety, there are big questions about the future of the planet itself. Though some still question the reality of global warming, all the signs are that something is happening to the climate as seasons change in ways that could hardly have been predicted a generation ago. Politicians right across the world now recognize that if we continue to ignore this issue, there could be a catastrophic collapse of the global economy within a couple of generations, not to mention increasingly hostile physical conditions facing us on a daily basis. When we add to this mixture the burgeoning population growth in some parts of the world, then it is no wonder that many people are seeing this as the heralding of global chaos. Contrary to some popular perceptions, it is younger people who find themselves most affected by this. Among people in their twenties today the level of depression is ten times greater than for those born before 1915, even though that generation lived through multiple major traumas. Something like 20 per cent of all teens and twenty-somethings may be suffering from depression, though some researchers put the figure as high as 50 per cent. This apparent rise may be due in part to a higher level of reporting of mental illness, though that is unlikely to explain it all, and in any case the statistics only include depression that is medically diagnosed and treated. Over and above that, many people just feel miserable. Even younger children are affected, with measurable anxiety levels among 'normal' schoolchildren now higher than those found in child psychiatric patients in the 1980s.[32] This widespread – and growing – sense of fearfulness is a bigger challenge than many Christians appreciate, not only because it is widely believed that Christianity has played a significant part in stirring up inter-religious strife and promoting environmental carelessness, but also because we seem not to have any meaningful eschatology that can speak into the situation. What Alan Roxburgh and Fred Romanuk say about local churches applies just as much (if not more) on a grander theological scale:

> the most important currency a congregation has to spend is hope . . . In many congregations the hope account is low and the cupboards of hope are getting bare.[33]

The re-imagination of a relevant biblical eschatology should be a top priority for today's Christians. For the whole of human history, the earth itself has been the one thing that could be relied upon to be stable in the midst of changing philosophical and political understandings. Now even that underlying certainty is being challenged, is it any wonder that people are questioning almost everything else?

Historical perspectives

It is easy enough to identify how people experience the cultural change that is now going on. But is there a bigger picture that might help to put it in context, and identify some of the reasons for our present anxieties? I have already indicated that I think framing this as a modern/post-modern disjunction may not be the most useful way of expressing it, if only because the diversity of terminology within that conversation is now so great that it is not easy to find a way of speaking of it that will command a wide consensus. Yet whatever label we attach to it, no one will deny that life today is quite different from how it was in the past.

In his book *A Whole New Mind*, Daniel H. Pink proposes an alternative way of looking at cultural change, which I believe offers some important insights into the challenges now facing the Church.

In common with other cultural analysts, he identifies three ages through which Western culture has evolved – the Agricultural Age, the Industrial Age, and the Information Age – but then adds a fourth one which he believes we are now entering, the Conceptual Age. Though his focus is on the culture of the Global North, which he treats in a linear fashion as having moved successively through these various stages, the taxonomy can – with qualifications – be used to illuminate trends in countries throughout the world. In reality, of course, cultural change has never proceeded in a narrowly linear fashion. Moreover, the notion of a single entity that can be labelled 'Western culture' is itself an ambiguous category. Within any given country, there is not one culture, but many, and there may even be different cultures existing side by side in close geographical proximity to one another. Rural Pennsylvania offers a striking example of this, where the Amish and their primitive lifestyle that is devoid of anything that might connect them to the wider world exist side-by-side with all the sophistications of contemporary consumerism. Even beyond such specific cultural enclaves, a country the size of the USA encompasses many different cultures, and depending on where you look, it can be an agricultural, and an industrial, and an information economy all at the same time. The same thing is true in Britain, while parts of the Global South are experiencing in this generation the sort of cultural shifts that took place over centuries in the Global North. With these qualifications, though, Pink's taxonomy still offers a useful reflective tool.

The *Agricultural Age* refers to the sort of rural economy that may ultimately be traced back to our most primitive hunter-gatherer ancestors. It was (and is) a world in which people live in harmony with nature, if only because the cycle of the seasons, and the amount of daylight there may be at given times of the year, determine the pattern of life that is both possible and appropriate. Though there may well be feudal overtones, this way of life (especially in farming as distinct from, say, fishing) has generally been an egalitarian one, if only because the workplace is also usually the home. There is something for everyone to do, and while there may be some social differentiation in terms of who does what, there is a creative and worthwhile role for each member of the family, including children. The idea that certain individuals will 'go to work' to support the others makes no sense here, for each person's skills (whatever they might be) are valued as an important contribution to the economic well-being of the family unit. Along with this there has generally been a wider sense of community, as people engaged in the same sort of work lived alongside one another, worked together, and therefore formed natural bonds of friendship. In this sort of cultural context, worship was part of everyday life and reflected an already-existing sense of community. It is still perfectly possible to find places where this is the case, in locations as far removed from one another as rural New England and the Highlands of Scotland, and at many points in between. Here, where people live and work alongside each other every day, what happens in church on Sundays serves to bless this shared life. Indeed, it was in this type of cultural context that what we now recognize as a service of worship had its origins. It works for people who already know one another. They do not need to interact in church, because they spend the rest of the week doing that, and such congregations can be fiercely resistant to practices that urban churches may regard as essential, such as sharing meals in the church, or even having a cup of coffee together after a service. But when churches in a different cultural environment try to operate by replicating these same patterns of worship, they soon find themselves faced with big challenges.

The *Industrial Age*, which in Britain dates back to the early eighteenth century, saw lifestyles become disconnected from the rhythms of the natural world and reorganized around the working hours dictated by industrialists, a change that was facilitated by one of the early products of the industrial revolution, namely the manufacture of gas from coal and the consequent invention of artificial lighting. But this change was merely cosmetic when compared with the more extensive alterations in human relationships that were brought about by the development of industrial processes. The industrial revolution was driven by coal and iron, which by definition were centred in mines and factories, and which in turn valued physical strength over and above other skills. This inevitably established a priority for male workers, and in the process marginalized the things that women might otherwise have contributed, while the mass-produced output of the factories required (and therefore helped to create) a new breed of consumers who would purchase the products. Instead of an economy based on skill (which therefore valued everyone), society moved to an economy based on money (which inevitably prioritized those who were in a position to make it). Out of this emerged a situation in which it would soon seem normal that men should be workers and producers, and women should be home-makers and consumers. So the industrial nuclear family came to birth, along with more privatized lifestyles as families migrated to urban centres where they knew no one else and were left to create their own spaces within which the family could survive in a place with no inherited sense of community. This was not the whole picture, of course, for many women (and even children) from impoverished circumstances ended up working in mines and factories. Nor were all industrialists blind to the importance of sustaining community, and some of them built model villages – even entire towns or cities – around their factories. But as a generalization, the Industrial Age and its associated urbanization led to the demise of more traditional ways of being.

Worship in this context often became a political issue, as workers either adopted, or reacted against, the religious preferences of the factory owners. This was the context in which (in Britain at least) the nature of Christian worship began to be redefined in different ways, as new forms of church emerged, represented most notably by Methodists, Congregationalists, and Baptists, but also including other smaller groups, all of them offering a way of being church that met the needs (educational as well as more narrowly religious) of those who might otherwise have been disadvantaged.

The Industrial Age survived in the West for 200 years and more, but by the late 1980s it was being displaced by the *Information Age*. The invention of the computer, and then subsequently the evolution of the worldwide web, created a 24/7 workplace that paid no attention to the artificial construct of 'working hours', still less to the cycles of nature. In this world, work could be wherever a computer was connected to a phone line. The skills required by heavy industry now looked like something from the age of the dinosaurs, for knowledge and mental agility became the key to the future. Physical mobility suddenly took on a whole new meaning, and the population movements of this period rivalled the move to the cities of the Industrial Age. By now the traditional family structures were in a state of disintegration, which made mobility a lot easier than before, because moving away from a set of fragmented relationships can generally be regarded as a gain rather than a loss. This was the generation when friends became the new family – and a whole host of TV programmes came to birth around that theme. Within this context, regular involvement in any sort of religious institution was becoming less common, but insofar as worship still featured in people's lives it became very much a matter of personal preference. This was partly due to the increased mobility of the age, and the explosion of choice that came about once people were prepared to travel some distance to go to church. Obligation was replaced by consumerism, and rules and regulations were pushed aside in favour of a concern for the personal well-being of the individual worshipper. This shift can easily be documented by looking at hymns and Christian songs that were written at the time, especially those originating from within an evangelical context, many of which have very little to say about God but a great deal of emphasis on an individual's quality of life, both interior and exterior. Some churches realized that in a consumer culture, the Church is in competition with other things for a share of people's time, and took steps to market themselves. But most did not, because they assumed that the social conditions of the Agricultural or Industrial Ages still prevailed and people would still exhibit a natural allegiance to the church of their forebears. The shift that took place at this time, from the consumption of goods to the consumption of experiences, is one that most churches have still not understood, even though it is at the heart of the apparent popularity of 'alternative' spirituality and the corresponding lack of appeal of the traditional church. Churches have tended to dismiss this by blaming the ideological construct of 'secularization', as if that alone can explain why Christians are struggling in the marketplace of spirituality, which ought to be their natural habitat. As a result, not only do Christians often miss the fact that 'secularization' is another dubious category that is now being seriously questioned by some of the same social scientists who originally proposed it,[34] but they also miss a key question in relation to their own missional prospects in this situation. For there is a considerable body of evidence from many countries suggesting that the reason for non-participation in the life of the Church is not intrinsically related to beliefs or religious experience – or secularization – but is rooted in the institutionalized nature of the Church, which has become disconnected from the realities of people's lives to such an extent that the Gospel itself looks like a foreign product, packaged in some alien environment to meet the needs of a society that is quite different from what we know and experience. The Australian writer Robert Gallagher offers wise advice with his admonition that

> Too many churches do not include essential cultural concerns in their Christian faith. Church life ... must be grounded in the experiences, attitudes, and reflection of its people if they are going to embrace the church.[35]

Not only may the polarization implied by language that contrasts the religious and the secular be less than the whole story: it may not be part of the real story at all. I remember at the turn of the millennium reading *The Experience Economy* by the Harvard business professors B. Joseph Pine and James H. Gilmore, in which they offered would-be entrepreneurs advice as to what sort of business might thrive and make the most money in the twenty-first century. They suggest that in a consumerist culture, people are looking for

> experiences to learn and grow, develop and improve, mend and reform ... [such] transformations turn aspirants into a 'new you', with ... ethical, philosophical, and religious implications ... We see people seeking spiritual growth outside the bounds of their local, traditional place of worship ...[36]

At the time, this struck me as a great description of the business that the Church is supposed to be in. Yet very few church leaders could see the possibilities, which no doubt partly explains the frequently voiced interest among key sections of the non-church community in being 'spiritual' but not 'religious'. It is certainly more than merely ironic that the authors of *The Experience Economy* also directed readers to the model that they felt would best serve the establishment of such enterprises – and found it in the New Testament concept of divine grace as the ultimate transformational tool for people seeking truly life-enhancing experiences![37]

By comparison with what the Global North is now experiencing, the lifestyles and challenges of these three cultural paradigms all appear to be deceptively simple and straightforward. Agriculture, of course, still exists, but Britain is no longer able to produce enough food to feed its population, and even the USA imports significant quantities of foodstuffs from other parts of the world. Industrial work still exists in pockets, though the heavy industries such as coal-mining and steel-making have almost completely disappeared as large-scale operations. The jobs have all gone east, to India, China, and other parts of Asia, and those engineering factories that are left now depend on importing their materials. Moreover – and surprisingly – information technology seems to have peaked, and many jobs in that sector have also been exported, mostly to the same countries as heavy industry. The specific details of how this is happening vary from one country to another, but these trends are widespread in the countries of the Global North. Daniel Pink calls this time the *Conceptual Age*. This reconfiguration of society is painful for many, especially those whose employment disappears. But it also comes at a time when Western people are better off than ever before. Being a millionaire has become so common that no one bothers to count them any more. Even those who are not quite so well off are still much richer than the generations that immediately preceded us. One of the major growth industries of the last ten years has been the building of self-storage facilities, where individuals can rent space to store stuff for which they have no immediate use, but which they do not wish to dispose of. We have so many possessions that the number of rooms in the average house is double what it was in my grandparents' day – and that at a time when more homes than ever are occupied by only one person!

This might all sound like the Promised Land, and to many of the world's people that is just what the Global North is. Why else would so many of them be so desperate to settle in these countries, often risking their all to gain entry by illegal means when their applications for residency are turned down? The underlying cultural reality is quite different. Far from being in paradise, many people find themselves economically well off, but trapped in a living hell of personal insecurity. Nor is this just an individual matter: the entire culture is increasingly unsure of itself and no longer knows whether to believe in its own rhetoric, or indeed whether there is any such thing as belief. A hundred years ago, our forebears were brimming with confidence about their own potential. The world quite literally was at their feet, and it seemed as if nothing would stop the expansion of the Western world and its power base. Though the days of empire and colonialism are now but a distant memory, economic expansion has continued through the exploitation of global marketplaces and the export of consumerism. But whereas in the past, Western people truly believed in the superiority of their own insights (which explains the evangelizing zeal with which they were promulgated), our culture has undergone a significant loss of confidence in itself – not least because the promise of world peace held out at the beginning of the twentieth century turned out to be hollow, and as time passed every horror surpassed the previous ones for brutality and inhumanity. By the 1960s, the self-confident worldview that had driven the Western mind for a thousand years or more looked decidedly jaded, if not altogether discredited. Today, it feels more and more like a favourite sweater that is unravelling, but which we find difficult to part with. We know that in its present form it is unserviceable, yet we are conscious of the fact that there is a lot of good material in the frayed strands, and not everything about the Enlightenment was bad. Where, after all, would we be without modern medicine and its antibiotics and anaesthetics, or the literacy and educational opportunities that continue to transform the lives of those who would otherwise never achieve their full potential? Or, for that matter, the worldwide web, which is as thoroughly Western a technological invention as anyone could imagine?

The religious side of this historic expansionism was, of course Christendom – indeed, Christendom was the original form of Western imperialism. Among church people the question of Christendom has dominated much recent writing – what it was, or might still be, and whether it was a good thing or a bad thing. Opinions vary, with some writers engaging in deep self-examination and regret for what can be seen as the extravagances of the past, while others (from different ecclesial traditions) parade themselves as being largely immune from criticism and therefore potential saviours for a post-Christendom generation. The reality is rarely so simple, of course, and it seems to me that we all struggle to one degree or another with the realities of our history. Some of our struggles are hardly justified, and in particular I find myself with an ambivalent attitude toward the high level of criticism that is now being aimed at our forebears in faith. It is a matter of incontrovertible fact that those who presided over the Church during the period of its cultural dominance engaged in or condoned some activities that were less than a faithful reflection of the Gospel. We might think of the Crusades, the Inquisition, the slave trade and, depending on whose analysis is followed, the missionary movements of the late nineteenth and early twentieth centuries. But to highlight such failures is merely to observe that the fate of the Church has always been in the hands of ordinary mortals who are liable to make errors of judgement, even on occasion to be self-serving and arrogant. Moreover, many of those events were happening anyway, for economic and political reasons that were nothing to do with religion. No doubt it would have been better if the Church had been less compliant, but that is human nature. I can only speak for myself, but I have a strong feeling that if I had been there in the same historical circumstances, it is highly likely that one way or another I would have been complicit in the same sort of behaviour.

Back in the 1990s, I worked on several occasions with the renowned Chinese missiologist Raymond Fung. During the period when he was Evangelism Secretary for the World Council of

Churches, we collaborated on several ecumenical Schools of Evangelism that brought together church leaders from around the world, with the intention that they might learn from each other as well as being stimulated by input from the two of us.[38] On each occasion some 30 to 40 people gathered for an extended period which, in one case, was as long as three weeks. Even before we had met any of the participants, it was taken for granted that many, if not all, of the leaders from Global North churches would bring a huge burden of guilt and remorse for the ways in which they believed their forebears had exploited and generally oppressed the participants from other nations. Sometimes this was well deserved. One of the most memorable moments from that series of events happened in Scotland on 17 June 1991. That was the date when the white South African government under F. W. De Klerk took the momentous decision finally to repeal its hated apartheid laws. Among the participants at the WCC event was a white bishop of the Anglican Church in South Africa, along with several black church leaders from that and neighbouring African countries. It was coincidental – though fortuitous – that our worship on that night was focused on the sort of prayer that consists of 'sighs too deep for words' (Rom. 8:26), in the course of which we all knelt around a tree branch and hammered nails in not-so-silent worship. There were many tears – of sadness for the atrocities of the past that had been committed in the name of Christ, but also of forgiveness and joy as a white man was embraced by black Africans who had suffered so much. Not surprisingly, those of us who were white felt blameworthy in some way, even if we had never been to South Africa or shared the theological or political opinions of its government. I remember Raymond subsequently reminding us that, notwithstanding our justifiable sorrow, the relationship between Christendom and the rest of the world had not all been negative, and we should grow up and stop beating ourselves up all the time. He pointed to the many positive things that Western adventurers had done to improve the lives of others through selfless service, and highlighted the fact that he himself owed a great deal to Christians from the Global North who had facilitated his education and provided him with opportunities that a Chinese person of his generation might never otherwise have had. Other, more cynical commentators have noted that Western people are questioning the accomplishments of science and technology (and, in the name of environmental protection, trying to scale them back) at the very point when other nations are in a position to take advantage of them, and the commentators have wondered if this is not motivated by the same sort of selfishness that we now complain about in the colonial era. No wonder our entire culture is suffering from a corporate lack of confidence in its own heritage. It is not my purpose here to whitewash Christendom, but to point out that – like most things in life – it has been a mixed blessing rather than an unmitigated disaster in all respects. But neither should we suppose that the anxiety now experienced throughout the culture is entirely disconnected from the attitudes of those who have gone before us. In the obituaries section of the final issue of *The Economist* for the twentieth century, there was just one entry: God! Belief in God, it suggested, had died because people 'nationalised God', 'reformers privatised him', and 'Christians turned not cheeks but swords against Muslims', and the result was 'the cynical, questioning, anti-authoritarian West'.[39] This striking claim highlighted something that seems to me to be of particular importance in relation to a Christian apologetic, namely that the present loss of confidence (at least as perceived by ordinary people in the street) is based more on practical concerns than on any great crisis of philosophical understanding. The theologian Thomas Oden put his finger on something important when he wrote:

> Not some theory but actual modern *history* is what is killing the ideology of modernity ... While modernity continues blandly to teach us that we are moving ever upward and onward, the actual history of late modernity is increasingly brutal, barbarian, and malignant.[40]

All things are interconnected, of course, and it is because the worldview that failed to deliver a better experience for the world's people was ultimately based on a rational understanding of the universe that rationality itself has come to be questioned as a reliable basis for making informed choices about human flourishing – including spirituality. This realization has played a big part in creating an environment in which it seems reasonable to take seriously ideas that in a previous age would have been dismissed as primitive and nonsensical. When you add to this our increased awareness of cultures other than our own, brought about by the expansion of the mass media and the growth of cheap travel, and then throw in a dash of natural human curiosity, you have the soil in which new forms of globalized spirituality can take root and grow.

For every person who is self-consciously looking for spiritual solutions, though, many more are just paralysed by fear. The challenges facing young people especially have been mentioned earlier. Church analysts have adopted more enthusiastically than other social commentators the language that would identify individuals by reference to their date of birth. The terminology of Generation X, Y, Millennials, and other slick labels, would be familiar to most church youth workers today. But the reality in the lives of young people is more complex than that – not to mention the fact that some researchers regard these categories as not being age-related at all, but as representative of a particular way of seeing things and of processing information. While I was writing this book, I was in a meeting with colleagues at Fuller Seminary where there was some discussion about the nature of theological education in the twenty-first century, and particularly whether the major responsibility for effective learning should rest with the students or the professors. One faculty member who is in his forties commented that the educational scene had changed even in the time that had elapsed since he completed his own graduate education some ten years previously. He observed that whereas in the past, a graduate school (as distinct from an undergraduate college) could have expected to enrol only mature adults, his own experience today was suggesting that maturity is no longer age related, and for many people adolescence now seems to extend into their thirties.

Others have wondered if, just as the twentieth century identified adolescence and teenage as key stages of life, maybe in the twenty-first century we will come to regard young adulthood as a separate stage, with its own challenges and opportunities. Whatever label we might care to use, it is certainly the case that the anxieties and fears, and the uncertainties about identity and relationships that the textbooks on developmental psychology would traditionally have placed in the teenage years, are not hard to find in people who are significantly older than that. In particular, such young people do not find it easy to connect either with church or with those forms of 'alternative' spirituality that their parents' generation seems to find so appealing. Their ways of dealing with the discontinuities of life are more basic, even elemental. In her study of the lives of young adults, psychologist Jean M. Twenge reminds readers that 'Being young has not always carried such a high risk of being anxious, depressed, suicidal, or medicated.'[41]

Older people, and civic authorities, regularly complain about what they regard as the anti-social behaviour of the young, especially when it manifests itself on the streets after long nights out in bars and clubs. But we need to ask why so many people regularly go out at weekends with the specific intention of getting drunk with alcohol or stoned through drugs. Hedonistic behaviour is not always happy behaviour, but often masks a deep uncertainty about fundamental questions of human existence. In lives filled with so much pain, drink or drugs at least offer the prospect of some relief from the harsh realities of life, even if it is only for a short period. In his book *Penguins, Pain and the Whole Shebang*, John Shore recounts his own remarkable experience of becoming a Christian without any connection with or intervention by the Church. He also offers the perspective of a recent convert on how he imagines God might see things (the tongue-in-cheek sub-title of the book is *Why I do the things I do, by God*). In the course of these musings, he puts his finger on a profound reality when he comments that 'a person without hope is, or always becomes, more animal than human'.[42] When people in the street (or politicians) behave in what seem like sub-human ways, it says something significant about our culture, afflicted as it is by a profound sense of futurelessness, and therefore hopelessness.

Two challenges for Christians stand out in particular. There is a theological question. Hope is at the heart of the Gospel, and yet no Christian tradition seems to have any sort of serviceable eschatology for the twenty-first-century world in which we live. Though they can still find resonances among some Christians, the opinions on this subject that originated in the millenarian speculations of the late nineteenth and early twentieth centuries are completely irrelevant to the concerns of the wider population. Yet most of us seem embarrassed to acknowledge any sort of eschatological dimension of faith, probably because we really have no idea what to think about it. This is something we need to work on: what would a meaningful twenty-first-century eschatology consist of? Besides that, however, there is also a missional question raised here. For if hedonism, with its accompanying and sometimes destructive indulgences, is the way in which many people confront and deal with life today, then in one sense that set of behaviours and rituals actually is their spirituality. What would it mean for that to be transformed and redeemed? This is not a silly question. As a matter of fact, I made a start on addressing it in a paper delivered to a conference in Windsor several years ago, and I have continued to reflect on it ever since.[43] It will surface again later in this book, as it is a key missional question that I believe we need to address in respect of many different aspects of contemporary culture. If we believe that this is God's world, and God is at work in it (the *missio Dei*), and if we further accept the most obvious consequence of this belief – that there can be no cultural no-go areas for God – then that must mean God can be found even, maybe especially, in the midst of all our struggles to be fully human. At heart, that is a question about relationships – with God, with the cosmos, with society, and with ourselves. These themes will surface repeatedly in the chapters that follow.

2 COMMUNITY

In this chapter I want to consider more specifically the impact of cultural change on the way we all experience life and find our place in the wider context in which we live. Like so many things that we aspire to, 'community' is not easy to define very precisely. We know it when we experience it, and suffer from its absence when we are deprived of it – but identifying what it might look like is a far more difficult matter altogether. One thing that is certain, though, is that significant numbers of people throughout the world feel that their lives are impoverished because we have somehow lost the capacity to create and sustain effective community. Movies, novels, and TV all reflect the sense of alienation that many of us feel. Our obsession with soap operas and reality TV programmes is part and parcel of this, as people whose own lives are empty search for meaning by connecting with other life stories as a way of discovering where they belong. There is always a hope that life-giving relationships will flourish, and yet in the end we know that most participants in such programmes will find themselves damaged and rejected rather than enriched. And we watch it all with such intensity precisely because it offers a commentary on our own lives. The viewers suffer with those who are rejected, not just in a general way, but because the seeming impossibility of creating and sustaining meaningful relationships is not a fiction but mirrors our own everyday struggles. The competitors in the numerous versions of talent contests in singing and dancing that can now be seen all around the world become, in effect, ritual scapegoats for us all. They carry our hopes and aspirations and, when they fail or are rejected, their downfall somehow makes our own daily struggles for meaning a bit more bearable. This sense of discontinuity is captured perfectly by Abe, a character in one of Douglas Coupland's novels who explains his motivation for wanting to join the corporate world by claiming that it will give substance to his life because 'People without lives like to hang out with other people who don't have lives. Thus they form lives.'[1] Coupland, as the narrator, then adds this telling comment: 'Even better, he'll have *company*.'

This phenomenon is no longer limited to the countries of the Global North: the nature of community is changing rapidly all over the world today, for a variety of different reasons. It is not so very long ago that people in the Global North looked with envy to the indigenous cultures of other continents, with their close-knit family groups in which the wisdom of the elders was passed on to the rising generations in a seamless way that had not changed for centuries. The relative poverty of such peoples in economic terms seemed to be more than compensated by the integration of all aspects of their life and work. There are, of course, communities that still live like that, but their prospects for future survival are diminishing all the time. One of the biggest threats is globalization, in all its many forms, most notably the spread of ideas through the expansion of the worldwide media and the internet, and the knowledge of other lifestyles that may seem more attractive than the one that any given individual now enjoys. The sort of economic migration unleashed in recent years through the expansion of the European Union to include former Eastern Bloc countries, or the constant stream of people entering the USA from Latin America, is just a small part of a global phenomenon, as marginalized people everywhere seek new opportunities to gain what looks like a better life. Economic migration moves in many different directions: from east to west and south to north, and with multiple regional variations. Alongside this, and somewhat paradoxically, those who have been economically successful in the rich North find themselves hankering after the simpler lifestyles from which these other people are trying to escape.

There is a good deal of idealized romanticism in both these movements. Poor people find that the prosperous countries to which they migrate are not always the Promised Land that they were led to believe. For some, it is never going to be paradise because they or their relatives borrow money from criminal gangs and as a result end up in a form of twenty-first-century slavery. Others merely find themselves lonely and without friends in places where they understand little of the language and even less of the structural systems of the culture. Conversely, rich people who imagine they might like to have a tribal existence in a rainforest would soon find the experience restrictive were they to try it – though that does not deter them from attempting to create their own version of what they imagine a simpler life to be, through using products from these isolated communities in the form of medications and so-called 'alternative' therapies. When we add into this picture the reality of the AIDS epidemic in many parts of the Global South, notably Africa, with its devastating impact on existing community life that is wiping out entire generations of people, it is clear that the whole question of who relates to whom, and how we do it in life-giving and nurturing ways, is not just a localized question but a matter of global concern. And this is before we have even mentioned religious controversies of one sort and another that are continuing to drive wedges between different sections of the world's peoples, reminding us that some individuals have no desire to be in community with others, and will go to extreme lengihs to oppose any form of global integration.

Community, culture, and change

In light of all this, it is no exaggeration to suggest that the one big question facing us today is the redefinition of community. In the Global North, the fragmentation of relationships is now taken for granted as a normal part of life. Some people have more sexual partners in a year than their grandparents would have had holidays in an entire lifetime, yet still persist in forging new relationships because, in their heart of hearts, they believe that acceptance and commitment is yet possible.

In the last chapter, I drew attention to Daniel Pink's taxonomy of cultural change using the notion of four successive Ages – Agricultural, Industrial, Information, and Conceptual.[2] As was noted there, in some places these different ways of being still exist in more or less pristine form (especially the Agricultural and the Industrial), while elsewhere one may be dominant but alongside elements of some of the others. Nevertheless, as a general overview of the story of Western (and increasingly global) culture, it offers a useful model for reflecting on some key issues, not least the ways in which our experience of community has changed. This is especially easy to trace by reference to the changing shape of the family from one age to another. In what has been characterized as the Agricultural Age, the primitive family was a building block of the community, offering its members economic security, employment, socialization, and education, as well as a stable context for reproduction and survival of the family itself. The Industrial Age created an urbanized population, as workers and their families moved to where they could find employment, and in the process the family was reconfigured into its industrial nuclear form to become a servant of the community, requiring rationalization and the differentiation of gender roles within the family, not to mention its role in creating and maintaining the sort of consumer base that would buy the goods that were produced in the factories. In the Information Age, with its implicit promise that anyone could become anything they dreamed of, a different social context developed in which the family members had to become creators of their own individualized community, as variable working patterns loosened the ties between different family members, and the family itself often became a marketable product. Now in the Conceptual Age, we are seeing a redefinition of the very idea of a family, as more and more people live predominantly single lives, with little that previous generations might have identified as a family at all.[3]

This way of describing the changes in community is of course a generalization, and it is not at all difficult to think of specific examples that buck the trends. Even in developed countries like the UK or the USA, all four types can still be found without our needing to look too hard. But as a big-picture analysis of the state of community, it offers some significant insights. The most obvious sign of what is happening is to be seen in the enormous increase in singleness, and in single-person households. The 2001 UK census showed that 32 per cent of homes were at that time occupied by only one person, and 25 per cent of the population were single, with marginally more single women than men. But at that time it was projected that in ten years, or less, those figures would have risen to 40 per cent of all households and at least 50 per cent of the population. The US census of 2000 demonstrated a similar trend, with more than 40 per cent of the population being single, though only 25 per cent were living alone – something that is no doubt due to the greater propensity for Americans to share accommodation with others with whom they are otherwise unrelated, and which is driven as much by personality type as it is by economic factors. However we look at it, more people today are more lonely than ever before. Some of this is a consequence of the long hours we now work, which leaves no time for forging relationships, or just leaves people too tired to be bothered making the effort. It is also the case that the loneliness many experience can often be 'the flip side of freedom and putting ourselves first'.[4] The fictional character Bridget Jones resonates with so many thirty-somethings (men as well as women) because her story depicts the reality of their lives.[5] In major cities in the USA, it is now possible to sign up for 'cuddle parties' that offer experiences of non-sexual hugging to those who are starved of physical contact with other people.[6] Meanwhile, many of those who enter relationships expect them to last for no more than a few years at best, and the notion of a 'starter marriage' is no longer a chat-show joke, but just the way it is for many individuals.[7]

The sort of loneliness we are now experiencing is clearly more than just an absence of friends. It represents a seismic shift in our expectations of life and therefore of community. In the 1970s the sociologist Peter Berger and his colleagues Brigitte Berger and Hansfried Kellner coined the phrase 'the homeless mind' as a way of describing the personal alienation that was both a cause and a symptom of the cultural upheavals of the 1960s.[8] Tracing the influence of various manifestations of modernity (prominent among them being technology, bureaucracy, and the creeping rationalization of systems and structures), they describe a metaphysical crisis that has affected Western people so that we no longer know what our social 'home' looks like. This ground-breaking study not only highlighted the psychological hardships that were being inflicted on individuals as they tried to cope in a situation where even their own identity was no longer assured, but it also drew attention to some important consequences for the social fabric of traditional institutions. In previous epochs, cultural institutions were respected and regarded as trustworthy building blocks that formed an essential component of the good life. Individuals found purpose for their own lives through involvement in them. Not only did they serve to identify the role that anyone might fulfil in relation to the wider community, but they also gave meaning to the lives of individuals by placing them within this broader context.

Thirty years ago, it was only a limited section of the population that was asking these profound questions about the inherited cultural norms. Today, such disillusionment is widespread within Western populations and the demise of institutions can be traced in just about every aspect of life. I recently came across groups of people in rural Cambridgeshire (England), who are concerned for the future of their local pubs, because business has plummeted as a result of people living constantly in their own private space (whether work or home), and having lost all sense of commitment to the wider community. In a circumstance where people have no commitment even to go and socialize with others at a pub, it is not surprising that religious institutions have suffered more than most, not least because it is easier to ditch them than it would be to abandon political, financial, or other institutions that look as if they are more essential to civic life than matters of faith. The impact of pluralism has also played a part in this demise, though it has to be conceded that the behaviour of previous generations of church people over issues such as child abuse has certainly not helped. The result is that today the inherited religious institutions have come to be regarded as not just irrelevant, but implausible and unbelievable. At the same time, though, Berger pointed out that 'human beings are not capable of tolerating the continuous uncertainty (or, if you will, freedom) of existing without institutional supports',[9] and so those who find themselves ideologically 'homeless' and ungrounded in the universe tend not to abandon institutions, but create new ones by developing 'secondary institutions'. In spiritual terms, these are constructed from the only materials that are still available, namely, the interior self and its concerns, which goes some way to explaining the renewed emphasis on therapies and mystical experiences of one sort and another that typifies much of the spiritual landscape today.[10] We will return to this theme later. First, though, we need to consider some less esoteric aspects of the breakdown of community.

Moving houses: suburbs and cities[11]

With some qualification, the trajectory from Agricultural to Industrial to Information to Conceptual can also be described as a move from the countryside to cities to suburbs and back to the cities again. The correlation of the first two of these with the Agricultural and Industrial Ages is undisputed, as also is the connection between the Conceptual Age and the rise in popularity of city living, though the suburban lifestyle emerged somewhat earlier than the Information Age proper. Of course, as with other aspects of cultural change, in some places these shifts are taking place simultaneously today, though the overwhelming movement of people throughout the world is firmly towards the cities. According to the United Nations Population Fund, the number of people living in cities in Africa and Asia increases every week by approximately 1 million – and by 2030 the number of city inhabitants worldwide is projected to be more than 5 billion, or roughly 60 per cent of the total world population at that time.[12] Life in the ghettoes of industrial cities has always been tough, and the hardships suffered by migrants from the countryside at the time of the industrial revolution in Britain are legendary, with even young children being forced to work long hours in poor conditions. The same circumstances have often prevailed in other parts of the world at a similar stage of industrial development, and this is still the reality of life for many people who are living through the burgeoning industrialization of the Global South today. But it is frequently the case that, in spite of all the difficulties they routinely face, there can be a strong sense of community among people who live even in slum conditions. So while the nature of the community might be different in each case, agricultural and industrial lifestyles both have the capacity for sustaining circumstances in which the human spirit can flourish.

It was the rise of suburbs that first began to undermine existing forms of community in the Global North. Though there had been some previous experiments with suburban living, it was only after the end of World War II that this lifestyle really began to expand. It is not hard to see why.[13] In many cities in the UK, homes as well as businesses had been destroyed or damaged by bombing raids, and in other places people were living in cramped and unsanitary conditions. What better way to celebrate a new start – and reward the privations of the war years – than by building new and better housing for people? This was also a period when public transportation was improving in reliability, car ownership was expanding, and there was therefore less necessity for people to live near to the places where they worked. These factors, combined with the availability of land and the cash to buy it, led to large population movements in the 1950s and 1960s as people saw the prospects of having the best of all possible worlds: keeping their employment in and around the cities, while living in an environment that might be built up but still retained the feel of the countryside. While the specific catalysts for suburban expansion in North America were not identical with those operating in the UK, a parallel development was taking place there during the same period.[14] Western culture has always promoted a romantic image of the rural environment as a carefree place in which to bring up children, with plenty of space and fresh air, and the design of the suburbs held out the promise of all that, with the added benefit of modern conveniences. To preserve the illusion of country living, roads that could more easily have been straight were intentionally built with twists and turns in them, while trees were planted to give the impression of woodland landscapes, and the cul-de-sac was invented as a semi-private space at the end of a lane. Though a car was more or less essential for successful suburban living, in some places cars were restricted to their own space on roads that deliberately excluded pathways for pedestrians, while pedestrian paths were provided through grassy areas surrounded by bushes. To the early inhabitants of such places, who had often come from much lower-grade housing in the cities, it all seemed too good to be true. And it often turned out to be, as they realized that they had lost the community they once had but did not always know how to create a new one. I recall some of my own relatives being in exactly that situation in the late 1960s. What they failed to understand at the time was that the one thing they really appreciated – having their own private space – was part of the design plan that by definition would make the creation of community less easy than they might have imagined or hoped for. Having a lot of space surrounding the house can inhibit the creation of community, because every interaction with someone else needs to be intentional in a way that is not the case in other more crowded locations.

Even finding your way around in a suburb can be difficult, because there tend to be no outstanding landmarks of the sort that can be found in a city, and the design of the roads provides the only sense of direction – though even that can be hard to navigate when (as in many British suburban developments) this just consists of endless roundabouts and intersections, every one looking more or less the same as the rest. In spite of that, not having a car can lead to an exceedingly poor quality of life in this environment, and many people who moved to these locations when they were younger now find themselves isolated and lonely in later life for this very reason. Yet we persist in creating more and more private space to insulate us from other people. Today's suburban houses are advertised and sold not only on the basis of the space between one house and the next, but by emphasizing the amount of personal space that members of the same family can occupy. We demand enough space for children to be separated not only from their parents but from their siblings, and in order to accommodate different working patterns some builders are now constructing houses with more than one 'master' bedroom so that spouses no longer need to share the same space but can have the freedom to live their own lives without disturbing their partner. This trend is emerging as a way of dealing with other aspects of contemporary living that are themselves undermining community, even within the context of our most intimate relationships. Many couples find that their main method of daily communication consists of scribbled notes left on the fridge door or the kitchen counter, or text messages sent from cell phones, and when they do sit down to have a face-to-face conversation they are either too tired to make much of it, or find it all too easy to limit their verbal exchanges to arguments about who has worked the hardest during the day, and whose turn it is to carry out household chores. In this time-starved existence, intimacy is limited to romantic weekends as a short-term fix for a lifestyle that society forces upon us, but which can look as if it was designed for the express purpose of destroying meaningful community – which, of course, is what often happens.

The sense of fearfulness that seems to be sweeping through much of the Global North is another factor impinging on the loss of community, because it inclines people to avoid the public spaces where in the past we might have been able to meet others. So we spend more time than ever in our own private spaces, and easily become isolated by living in a place that was supposed to improve the overall quality of life. All age groups are affected by this. Older people who can no longer drive find it hard to go anywhere to meet others, while children can end up imprisoned in their own homes for fear of accidents, abductions, and the like. Meanwhile, their parents spend much of their lives cocooned in their own private spaces, driving from home to work without any interaction with another living soul. In some places suburban housing is built with the rear of homes facing the street, thereby increasing the isolation by making it possible to go straight from the main rooms of the home (which are typically facing out onto a private, enclosed garden), into the garage, and then to drive straight out into the road without once having stepped outside the privatized environment. Unlike the city, which has space for everyone on its streets, suburbs were designed to exclude strangers, and a stranger in a suburb will always be a potential criminal. But the design of much housing in effect ensures that everyone is a stranger to everyone else, because nobody meets anyone else unless they are intentional about doing so. The ubiquitous creation of 'Neighbourhood Watch' schemes is a sure sign of the non-existence of community: nobody knows anybody else, so it has become necessary to create a bureaucratic system that will identify and marginalize strangers.[15]

Many of the original conditions that led to the construction of suburbs no longer exist, and consequently there is a new openness to different ways of living. One of the manifestations of this is to be seen in the way that people are moving back to the city again. Cities are being rebuilt in imaginative ways, with old factories and warehouses being converted into apartments, and other forms of new housing growing up alongside this regeneration. Places that once had virtually no resident population are becoming vibrant neighbourhoods – but the shape of those neighbourhoods, and the way that people relate to one another within them, is yet another challenge to some inherited notions of community. The city has always had an attraction for lonely people, if only because it is impossible to be in a city without being in the presence of others. Even if you have no idea who any of them are, the mere fact of being part of a crowd can itself impart a sense of belonging to a bigger group. But this opportunity to meet strangers is not the only attraction offered by city living. There is also the accessibility of public space that belongs to everyone, whether in the street life of classic city squares and piazzas or the more homely ambience of a contemporary coffee shop. Cities also generally offer a visually stimulating environment, with the architectural beauty of older buildings alongside contemporary examples of civic art. Then there is the fact that once the size of a place has reached a certain point, it generates its own critical mass that facilitates the emergence of creative enterprises of many kinds, including (usually) a vibrant local economy. In a suburb you may have to travel miles to find a shop; in the city you are unlikely to have the same problem.

But the migration of populations to the cities of the Western world is not a return to the urban lifestyles of the past. Partly as a result of the absence of facilities such as schools, city life is coming to be characterized by the emergence of 'urban tribes' consisting largely of adults. Though this terminology has only become widely used in recent years,[16] the trend toward new forms of communal connectedness that would go beyond traditional family relationships had already been identified by Peter Berger and his colleagues in the 1970s, and they used the word 'tribe' to describe this phenomenon.[17] What started as a counter-cultural movement among more or less fringe people in the 1960s has now become widespread in society, as we are all now more likely to define our social identity by reference to various sub-cultures that adopt a particular set of interests, beliefs, and ethical values. An extensive account of this new tribalism in relation to the city has been offered by Ethan Watters, based on research with more than a thousand members of such 'tribes'.

Though his interviewees consisted mostly of individuals in their twenties and thirties, it is more likely that the tribal lifestyle is defined less by age than by attitude and outlook, along with the unifying factor of the need to create a new life in an urban context. This sort of tribe typically emerges more or less spontaneously among individuals who happen to find themselves in the same place, but without any other pre-existing networks of significant friends or relatives. The vocabulary of emergence is actually a good way to describe this social reality. With origins in geometry and chaos theory, the concept of emergence is a way of identifying the phenomenon whereby a complex organization comes into being not as a result of a grand design promoted by a leader, but as a consequence of the collective actions of its relatively humble members.[18] Watters takes for granted Berger's definition of 'homeless minds': his starting point is the realization that many people today are 'facing the challenges of lives navigated without signposts',[19] but because of the fragmented individualism of the culture, the only way they can create meaning for themselves is by mingling with others who are in the same situation, and out of those interactions creating a new frame of reference that can provide a renewed sense of purpose and identity. Significantly, from a Christian perspective, he identifies this as the search for a story:

> A life ... is too complicated a thing to hold in the mind, and this is why we need to identify with stories of others living in our time. It is only through the sharing of these cultural narratives that we can give coherence and meaning to our existence ... important things in our own lives can go unseen or misunderstood if we lack the story template in our cultural vocabulary to describe them.[20]

Such spontaneous groupings offer the structure and discipline that many people have either lost or never had, not only through mutual accountability but also by the creation of new narratives of significance that might be drawn from something as seemingly trivial as the annual camping trip or as radically serious as vegetarian lifestyles or social action on behalf of the dispossessed and marginalized. Though it is early days in the repopulation of the cities of the Global North, this process looks like continuing for the indefinite future, and offers a different understanding of community spirit than the pattern inherited from the democratic civic structures of the first half of the twentieth century. It is often claimed that our growing sense of loneliness and individualism threatens social coherence because we are now less likely to engage in the sort of voluntary associations that in days gone by would have helped others.[21] But those who find themselves living in this context often migrate to the city from a prior suburban experience in their earlier life, and their awareness of the deficiencies of suburban living is informed by the knowledge that these places were created by well-meaning civic authorities. A typical reaction to this would be to question how something that contributed to a perceived problem can also contribute to its resolution, and therefore new forms of mutual accountability will be required. At its best, this emerging 'tribal' behaviour can be seen to be reinventing responsibility in a way that goes back to more ancient roots by offering the sort of support that originates in friendship, without the need for institutional structures to determine how such community ought to operate. Of course, networks of like-minded friends have the potential for becoming introspective and self-centred, but Watters' research revealed that many such groups are aware of that possibility, and take intentional steps to avoid it. The responses from the people he surveyed showed that they were as likely to be found selflessly helping others as being hopelessly self-indulgent – because 'the moral value of our lives was not in the nature of the activities we engaged in but in the friendships and group support that existed in and around them'.[22]

Church, community, mission

You would think that in a context where people are not only cut off from meaningful community, but know that they are and are desperate to find a better way, it would be a relatively simple matter for the Church to make significant connections with those who are presently beyond its borders. It would be, if the Church was anything like the sort of place commended by Stephen Cottrell:

> a safe and affirming environment where you know yourself to be valued and loved, where your questions are taken seriously, where you can grow at your pace and towards your own potential ... helping people to become part of a community and to understand themselves within that community.[23]

Unfortunately, things are nothing like so simple. In the 1970s, Peter Berger was able to claim with some justification that religious institutions were struggling more than other civic structures. The intervening years have put this in a different perspective for many people, and there is now enormous distrust of almost all inherited institutions, something that at one level should be good news for the Church in the sense that it is at least no worse than the worlds of politics, finance, and so on. Moreover, in terms of the core values of the Gospel, the Church ought to be in a position to connect with the existential aspirations of those who find themselves spiritually disconnected and searching for a new home. When you think about it, Jesus himself gathered the equivalent of an urban tribe, bound together not by traditional family ties but through a network of beliefs, lifestyle, and ethical commitment. When he was asked about his family, he responded by saying that 'Whoever does the will of God is my brother and sister and mother' (Mark 3:35). It is even likely that he was working in the context of an urban reconstruction taking place in first-century Galilee that, within its own frame of reference, had more than a few points of similarity with the regeneration of today's cities.[24]

Of course, the realities with which we are wrestling are more challenging than that. One of the reasons that so many of our traditional institutions have been brought into disrepute is because they appear to have denied their core values, and in this regard the Church is no exception. I remember being given a book by an American author some 30 years ago, with the intriguing title *Crowded Pews and Lonely People*. The author, Marion Leach Jacobsen (a Christian educator of a previous generation, who was certainly no militant rabble-rouser), wrote:

> Our churches are filled with people who outwardly look
> contented and at peace but inwardly are crying out for
> someone to love them … just as they are – confused,
> frustrated, often frightened, guilty, and often unable to
> communicate even within their own families. But the other
> people in the church look so happy and contented that one
> seldom has the courage to admit his own deep needs before
> such a self-sufficient group as the average church meeting
> appears to be.[25]

There has been remarkably little change in the meantime. As one person put it to me recently, 'My church has too many meetings but no real fellowship.' The journalist John Shore identifies this as a missional issue for today's churches when he asks:

Why are so many Christians so obnoxious and mean-spirited? It seems like Christianity's mostly about being judgmental, narrow-minded, and having an infuriatingly condescending attitude toward anyone who isn't a Christian. Christians are so busy being smug about being Christian that they forget to be kind.[26]

More than one piece of empirical research into the reasons why people leave churches has highlighted the same trend: for whatever reason, church as we know it seems to be a place where people can find real difficulty in being accepted.[27] The typical attitude of church leaders to this has been well described by Michael Riddell, Mark Pierson, and Cathy Kirkpatrick in their book *The Prodigal Project*:

The church accepts no responsibility for the increasing tide of disaffection, but rather wants to call into question the integrity of those who have been alienated.[28]

But to respond like this is a form of denial. I have a good deal of sympathy with such people, if only because I have experienced all this at first hand. In the year 2000, my wife and I moved to the city of Aberdeen, in north-east Scotland, leaving behind a church in Stirling that we had been involved with for 20 years or more. The geographical distance was not great (120 miles or so), but in terms of church life we might as well have moved to a different planet. Not long before our move, my wife had organized a massively successful interactive Christmas event that brought a sizeable percentage of the population of the city of Stirling into the church.[29] News of this had spread to some church leaders in Aberdeen, and she was invited to orchestrate a millennial project that culminated in a similarly huge Christian event that saw thousands of people on the streets to celebrate Pentecost Sunday 2000, complemented by a whole cluster of integrated events including storytelling workshops in local bookstores, a youth event in an ice-rink, a series of lectures by leading academics, and much more. That was the vision of the Regional Ecumenical Team, comprised of bishops and their equivalents in other denominations, but we soon found that church at a local level was quite different. Given my wife's accomplishments, and the worldwide reputation that both of us have earned as missionally adventurous leaders, you might have expected local churches to be queuing up to recruit either or both of us as honorary associate ministers to help them further their mission. Not only did it not happen, but most were openly hostile and one church told us not to bother thinking about joining them because they would never have us even as members! Prior to this, I could not have believed how difficult it might be to 'break into' a church. It still amazes me to think that churches with financial struggles would not welcome as many people as they can get, especially if they might be likely to be available for unpaid work in ministry. But if people who actually want to be part of a worshipping community meet with that level of resistance, what chance is there of churches like that ever connecting with those who have no prior connection with the Christian faith? In speaking of this with others, I have come to realize that such hostility is far from unusual, and is actually quite deeply ingrained in the attitudes of many Christian people. Tolerance of incomers – let alone showing friendship to them – is not even on their radar. If all this sounds a bit too self-indulgent, it should be noted that I am by no means the only person to be concerned about it. Jeff Astley, a highly experienced adult educator, identifies this as a major issue in relation to the spiritual nurture of believers, and insists that the sort of disaffection that can be found among many Christian people is not a matter of a 'trivial form of consumer dissatisfaction. It is a serious complaint about a serious shortcoming.' He goes on to add that 'Frankly, the churches just have too much junk in them.'[30]

These are strong words from a serious academic. I ought to add here that not all churches are like this, but a depressingly large number seem to be – and of all denominations and theological persuasions. No doubt there are many different explanations that could be given for the sense of alienation and rejection that even believers can experience. But in terms of the life of the church in the community, it all raises a very straightforward, but challenging issue. For if the Gospel is supposed to be about forgiveness, acceptance, and community – not to mention love, joy, peace, patience, generosity, faithfulness, gentleness, and self-control (Gal. 5:22–23) – then in too many instances there is a serious credibility gap between the product that seems to be on offer and the experience that is actually delivered. If even regular worshippers fail to find the values of the Kingdom being embraced among them, then what chance is there that those many lost people who are looking for meaningful community might find it within a Christian congregation? Churches are realizing that, whether we like it or not, in today's consumerist culture we need to do more than merely exist in order for people to recognize the contribution that faith in Christ might make to the enrichment of their lives. But what happens when the marketing is better than the product? The importance of social integrity as well as theological faithfulness is central to the New Testament. It was Jesus himself who made a direct correlation between meaningful mission and the quality of his disciples' relationships (John 13:35). There are many reasons why people might connect with the Church, but there is only one thing that encourages them to stay – and that is finding friends. The aphorism attributed to the late Carl W. Buechner is quoted so often because it conveys a message that is basic to all human interactions: 'They may forget what you said, but they will never forget how you made them feel.' And, of course, Jesus himself advised his disciples how to handle such situations (Luke 10:10–12).

In spite of that, there are still many good people in churches who struggle to reflect the sort of community they know to be at the heart of the Gospel. One factor in our apparent inability to create meaningful community is that we tend to assume some things about the Church that were once true, but can no longer be taken for granted. It is easy to imagine that those who gather for worship are automatically part of a community, just by virtue of their presence in the same time and place. In rural communities, that was always historically the case, as people lived and worked alongside one another and what took place in church on a Sunday was just another aspect of an existing web of relationships. Something similar would have been true at the time of the industrial revolution, when workers would typically have gathered in the churches that were built by their employers in order to service an existing community. There are places where it still works that way, most obviously in a rural context – though even here, the steady influx of incomers (mostly escaping from the suburbs) is affecting that pattern. But as a generalization, much of that innate connection between worship and the everyday life of the community has disappeared, and many folk in church know each other only as intimate strangers. In this context, it is counter-productive to imagine that those who gather for worship are a community, when clearly they are not by any ordinary definition. By insisting that they are we are just going to induce a sense of guilt because we feel we ought to know one another better than we do. We need first to work at creating community, before we can then celebrate it. Much of the *angst* in contemporary church life arises out of this lack, whether we think of arguments about worship styles, or discontent with over-rationalized structures and committees and the accompanying expectation that everyone should fit into some predetermined pattern. Most robberies taking place in fast-food outlets are committed by employees who feel aggrieved at the way they have been treated. It is worth pondering whether McDonaldized practices in church life might be producing angry people who through their non-existent, or sometimes abusive, relationships with others are undermining some of the core values of the Gospel. It is worth noting that a key concern for the apostles was to create churches in which believers could build each other up and nurture faith, and behaviour that violated this sense of togetherness (*koinonia*) was regarded as far more damaging than doctrinal differences.[31] The church that finds a way to address effectively the alienation, relational fragmentation, and personal lostness that now afflicts huge swathes of the population at all levels will make a major contribution to the life of the wider civic society, as well as becoming a place of personal nurture that would truly qualify to be 'the body of Christ'.

Reinventing spiritual community

Are there any models for church renewal? The answer is clearly yes, for the other side of the coin of church decline is that some churches are growing. Some grow as a result of people who are disillusioned with one church leaving to transfer their commitment to another one. Such people frequently take their disillusionment with them, and end up constantly moving from one congregation to another. Others are growing because they attract people from a wide geographical area who are looking for specialist ministries, which might be as diverse as good childcare, or a specific style of sermon, or a time of meeting that fits in with a particular lifestyle, or any number of other variables. All these things are, however, variations on a theme, and they take it for granted that the inherited pattern of gathering in congregations will be at the centre of church life. There is nothing wrong with this in itself, though it is worth noting that the sort of triumphalism represented in some contemporary forms of worship is unlikely to appeal to those who are genuinely searching for spiritual answers to life's questions. Not only can this be a form of denial of the struggles facing the Church in today's culture, but it also fails to connect with the reality of people's experience and the messy things that we all now struggle to deal with. This is not an issue that only affects those with no prior connection to the Church: I recently stood next to the wife of a denominational leader who was unable to sing any of the songs at a major church conference because, as she put it, 'this is not how it is – in my life, or anyone else's'.

Quite apart from such considerations, much traditional church life represents a way of being that struggles to address the underlying issues of belonging and community, which no doubt explains why so many churches that are patterned like this feel a need to add other activities such as home groups as a way of trying to make up for what they recognize as a deficiency. Beyond any of that, though, it is becoming obvious that the reinvigoration of Christian community along traditional lines is unlikely to be meaningful for anyone who is not already within the orbit of the Church, or who has no prior experience of congregational life. The study by Paul Heelas and Linda Woodhead of the spiritual life of the town of Kendal, briefly mentioned in the last chapter, exemplifies this.[32] Though Kendal was chosen for study largely because of its proximity to their own institution (the University of Lancaster), it is a fairly typical smallish traditional English community on the edge of the Lake District that could therefore be regarded as offering a snapshot into the spiritual concerns of ordinary people more widely. On the basis of their investigations there (which took place over a period of two years), they concluded that what they call 'the holistic milieu' (spiritual 'alternatives' of various kinds) more closely matches the spiritual aspirations of people than 'the congregational domain' (traditional church). They went on to offer the opinion that, as the congregational domain continues to decline and the holistic milieu grows, the two could be about equal in size before the middle of the twenty-first century.[33]

In order to reach others, whether in suburbs or city centre, there will have to be some entirely fresh thinking about the nature of community itself that takes account of the motivations that inform our corporate search for personal meaning. I have intentionally used the adjective 'corporate' there, rather than 'individual'. Though the phenomenon of Berger's 'homeless minds' is still very much a reality, one of the things that has changed since his original research is that today's 'homeless minds' are more aware of the fact that the search for meaning does not need to be exclusively individualistic and inward-looking, but must incorporate an element of relationality, with some recognition of the intrinsic interconnections not only between individual persons, but between people and the physical environment, and indeed the wider cosmos. Heelas and

Woodhead have offered the opinion that this is starting to come about through the emergence of new, secondary institutions that navigate a '"middle way" between primary [i.e. inherited, traditional] institutions and the fragile resources of the homeless self drawing upon itself'.[34] In reflecting on this, I naturally wondered if some new forms of church might actually correlate with this notion of a 'middle way'. Following the Church of England's report, *The Mission-Shaped Church*,[35] Anglicans and Methodists in England have joined forces to promote the establishment of 'Fresh Expressions' of church in their two denominations.[36] Though the town of Kendal offered examples of a wide variety of theological and ecclesiastical expressions within its congregational domain, they were all what a bishop recently described to me as 'stale expressions of church'. There was certainly nothing that could qualify as 'emerging church'. The use of this term tends to provoke very different reactions from Christian commentators and scholars, and I would be the first to acknowledge that it is a somewhat slippery term that clearly means different things to different people, and in different cultural contexts.[37] In that respect, it shares a problem of definition with a lot of other language that is commonly used to describe aspects of the contemporary spiritual search. It is sometimes applied as a description of any form of innovation in church life, even just a different congregation than what has been the conventional one in a given context. When adopted in that way, it becomes in effect a marketing slogan, offering a new packaging for what is likely to be an old product. Kester Brewin highlights the potential deficiencies in such an approach:

> My problem with many of these 'Emerging Church' projects is that they are still attempting to bring church up to date by 'train spotting' some aspects of culture and making church fit it. I want to argue that in the 'Emergent Church' the emphasis will be on being the train, rather than trainspotting: rather than trying to import culture into church and make it 'cool', we need instead to become 'wombs of the divine' and completely rebirth the Church into a host culture ... I think we need to advance with caution for fear of these things precipitating a revolution that will not last, and bringing changes that will just be tactical.[38]

As the quotation indicates, he proposes the use of the term 'emergent' to describe forms of Christian community that go beyond merely rearranging the pieces we now have. This hardly clarifies things, however, not least because the term 'emergent' is being widely used in North America in place of 'emerging', and therefore introduces another sort of ambiguity into the conversation.[39] I would also want to be less critical than he is of innovation that stays within the inherited framework of church as congregation: if the Gospel is to be embedded in the culture, then we need to recognize that while there are certain common threads, culture itself is to be found in many different shapes today, including a reinvigorated form of traditionalism. There is, in any case, a clearly identifiable strand within the 'emerging church' that does what Brewin is arguing for, by starting with an entirely blank sheet and attempting to reimagine the ways in which authentic discipleship might need to be expressed in order to have integrity within the changed and changing circumstances of contemporary culture.

The lack of clarity in terminology has led to divergent assessments of the reality it represents, with some traditional church leaders regarding the emerging church as the enemy of true faith at the same time as others are investing significant resources in promoting it. The American academic Don Carson has dismissed the movement as a perversion of the Gospel,[40] while Archbishop of Canterbury Rowan Williams has put his considerable theological weight behind the Fresh Expressions initiative, promoting the view that there will be multiple new ways of being church in today's culture, and what is required is a 'mixed economy' of old and new working in partnership with one another. It is doubtful whether they are actually referring to the same things, though. Dr Carson's critique seems to be directed against what in other circles might be labelled 'post-evangelicalism',[41] though even within that frame of reference it offers a somewhat detached analysis that takes no account of the praxis of actual church groups but focuses almost entirely on the writings of one American 'emergent' leader, Brian McLaren.[42] The archbishop, on the other hand, is concerned to promote a genuinely missiological engagement in which Gospel, Tradition, and Culture are brought together to address some fundamental questions, such as: How might we follow Jesus faithfully in today's post-modern culture? What might new wineskins for new circumstances look like? How can Gospel and Culture be brought into a creative dialogue that will affirm and challenge both of those conversation partners? This understanding of the emerging church is significant because it locates it precisely in that liminal place out on the fringe (from the Latin *limen*, meaning 'threshold') that is implied by the notion of the 'homeless mind'. Ben Edson, leader of one of the more long-standing and successful emerging churches within the Church of England,[43] has adopted the terminology of liminality as a way of understanding his own social context among the urban tribes of the city of Manchester, and finds it helpful to think of the emerging church as offering what the anthropologist Victor Turner called 'communitas', which for him was a way of describing the sort of experience that characterizes the corporate life of marginalized people in times of liminality:

> Since communitas arises out of situations of liminality, any church that engages with post-modernity (itself a culture of liminality) is by definition going to find itself in a situation of liminality.[44]

This all strikes a chord with the rise of the urban tribes, as well as correlating with the sense of loneliness experienced by many suburban people. It also connects with some central aspects of the ministry of Jesus, who was a liminal person *par excellence*, and whose example disciples are exhorted to follow (John 20:21). Indeed, Turner's description of liminality could easily have been modelled on biblical characters:

> Prophets and artists tend to be liminal and marginal people ... who strive with a passionate sincerity to rid themselves of the clichés associated with status incumbency and role-playing and to enter into vital relations with other men [*sic*] in fact or imagination.[45]

In their book *Emerging Churches*, Eddie Gibbs and Ryan Bolger include 'identifying with Jesus' as one of nine key marks of the emerging church.[46] It could be argued, however, that this is not merely one mark among many, but is the underlying foundation on which their other eight depend, and that this is one of the most significant contributions that the emerging church is making to the wider discussion of Christian community. It is certainly the case that their other key marks were also fundamental characteristics of the ministry of Jesus himself: transforming secular space, living as community, welcoming the stranger, serving with generosity, participating as producers, creating as created beings, leading as a body, and merging ancient and contemporary spiritualities. Jesus is central for the emerging church, not so much as an object of belief but as an example to be followed. This is a bigger shift than most commentators seem to appreciate. It goes well beyond any of the historic creeds, in which the entire life story of Jesus is subsumed into a single comma between statements about his birth and his death! It also moves beyond all the twentieth-century arguments about how – if at all – the historical Jesus might be a necessary underpinning for the Jesus of faith, and firmly aligns itself with the view that the New Testament Gospels are essentially biographical, offering hard information about Jesus as he actually lived and worked.[47] In particular, by taking seriously Jesus' teaching about the Kingdom of God, emerging Christians want to learn from the way in which Jesus related to other people, and follow that pattern inasmuch as they are able. Moreover, this is not just a return to the past, but a living reality for the present. The question is not the highly publicized bumper sticker, 'What would Jesus do?' but the more sophisticated theological question, 'What is Jesus doing?' To tell the story of Jesus in this way, rather than focusing on the theological meanings that have been attached to his life, death, and resurrection, represents a huge paradigm shift in Christian thinking. This subtle, but highly significant distinction, however, arises out of a thoroughly biblical notion, namely the concept of the *missio Dei* ('mission of God') as a way of understanding the work of God, and therefore the call of the Gospel. It was Karl Barth who in 1932 first proposed that mission should be understood as an activity of God, rather than as a church programme, though it was the mid twentieth century before the term *missio Dei* was coined.[48] Given the alienation from religious institutions felt by many people, but the intrinsic impossibility of giving up on the existential search for meaning and spiritual purpose, it is pragmatically sensible, as well as theologically necessary, that we stop asking what the Church is doing and move toward a renewed focus on what God is doing. The notion that this is indeed God's world, that God is at work in it, and that being the Church involves a call to discern where God is at work and to be intentionally aligned with that, is fundamental to much emerging-church thinking.

The extent to which all this will require us to think in different ways can hardly be exaggerated, and is likely to be more far-reaching than most of us now appreciate. There is a fundamental theological question underlying this that we need to address in a more thoroughgoing fashion than we have so far done. It is a bigger question than can be tackled here, and merely naming it will show why that is the case. Simply put, where do we get our models for what it means to be a community of faith centred on Christ? The classic answer, of course, is that we refer to our inherited ecclesiological understandings. Though such understandings vary enormously from one denominational tradition to another, the primary components feeding into such discussion are clear enough: Scripture and tradition. History plays a big part, as also (in my opinion) does personality type and individual preference. History has generally been seen as a subsidiary consideration that impinges on how we view Scripture and tradition, rather than being a formative influence in its own right. As was noted in the last chapter, there is now a widespread recognition that, culturally speaking, the days of Christendom are over, and Christians need to find different ways of relating to the wider society. What is not so often recognized is that the end of Christendom actually removes a key historical element that is deeply embedded in all our ecclesiologies. This is as true for the inherited ecclesiology of the Free Churches (Methodists, Congregationalists, Baptists, and so on) as it is for the Reformed, Anglican, and Catholic traditions. Whenever we define the Church from within our inherited ecclesiologies, we will always get a Christendom-shaped Church, because these traditional patterns are themselves a manifestation of Constantinianism, and in many cases their structures are all but identical to the governance of the Roman empire.[49] When the emerging church prioritizes Christology over against ecclesiology, it is being far more subversive of the *status quo* than most church leaders would like to admit. Moreover, it is being subversive in a way that calls us back to the fundamentals of Scripture by inviting us to rediscover our roots in the person of Jesus and to reshape Christian community in the light of his radical understanding of discipleship and of the Kingdom of God. In saying this (and unlike some others) I am not implying that we should adopt a cynical and negative attitude toward past generations of Christians, whether in the time of the Roman empire, or the Middle Ages, or for that matter the Reformers. Hindsight is a wonderful thing, and it is too easy to delude ourselves into thinking that we would have behaved any differently than our forebears did. Arguably, the very things that we now see as negativities in Christian history were actually an authentic contextualization of the faith within cultural circumstances very different from our own. At the same time, we should remember that the fundamental orientation of the Gospel is towards the future rather than the past. Ray Anderson

poses a challenging question when he asks, 'which century is normative for our theology?'[50] His answer to it is even more radical, for
he denies that any one century (even the first) might be normative,
and instead insists that in any authentically biblical theology there
must always be an 'eschatological preference' looking to the future,
and that this offers 'a biblical and theological paradigm for ministry
based on the liberating praxis of the Holy Spirit'.[51]

Dreaming an alternative future

Finally, then, we need to ask what this might look like in the context
of today's culture. How might our knowledge of Jesus and the
eschatological orientation of the Gospel nurture a generation that
yearns for new ways of belonging at a time when the traditional
foundations that sustained our forebears seem to be no longer either
credible or practical? Put another way, what might be the shape of a
new tribal community that will function as a Gospel-centred secondary institution along the lines of the 'middle way' identified by
Paul Heelas and Linda Woodhead?[52]

Organic and connected

Today, we are more aware than ever before of both our individual
loneliness in the world, and yet our interconnectedness with the
entire cosmos. In spiritual terms, a Gospel community is likely to be
following Jesus without regard for traditional denominational
labels. We are already seeing this in inherited forms of church, as
people join them not out of theological conviction but because they
feel at home in a given local context. Future generations of disciples
will be even less interested in denominations – not because they
reject them, but because they regard all of them as partial insights
into a message and way of being that is larger than any one of them
by itself. Spiritual disciplines will be adopted from across the
spectrum with scant regard for their origins, and will be merged to
form new ways of expressing faithful discipleship. This is likely to
take place not only across theological traditions but also across the
boundaries of time and space, so that insights from the Celtic saints
will be seamlessly melded with notions from medieval monasticism,
alongside biblical passages and insights from contemporary artists
and musicians. The search for connectedness will not, however, be
restricted to what might look like overtly 'religious' matters, but will

extend into areas of social justice and environmental care, as well as personal interior development, as the inherited division between the sacred and the secular is dissipated in favour of a more organic unity of all things. Following Jesus as a pioneer and icon of such wholeness will create spaces for authentic journeying with others who find themselves attracted by these values, backed up by a conviction that faithfulness is defined more by reference to a close walk with the Master than by membership in an organization. I will have more to say about this in the next chapter, as it seems to me to be a central matter in relation to Christian mission in today's world.

Spiritual and incarnational

As the wider culture diverged from the norms of Christendom, different groups of Christians gradually withdrew from meaningful engagement with it. People like the Amish, who eschew all contact with technological inventions, or the Shakers who have reduced their number almost to extinction by banning sex, may seem extreme, but the same trends can be found among many other groups. In the course of the twentieth century, being 'in the world, but not of it' became a mantra for many, who were fearful of connecting with the wider culture because they believed that God had in effect abandoned it, and retreated to some heavenly world instead.[53] The reasons for this isolationism can be debated, but the reality is all too evident and has arguably inflicted more damage on the mission of the Church than any amount of atheism or agnosticism from outside, for it ensured that a Christian voice in the public square was, at best, muted for much of the last century, and mostly unheard. We should be grateful for the fact that this mindset is very much a minority one today. Renewed emphasis on the *missio Dei* has played a big part in this, as also has a rediscovery of what it means for the Church to be like Jesus by being truly incarnational. It has enabled Christians to reaffirm that this is God's world, and therefore there can be no no-go areas for God, so even in the most inhospitable reaches of the culture God may be found at work. Alongside this is a fresh consciousness that some aspects of the culture may need to be challenged in the name of the Gospel, which is creating a new sense of the importance of spiritual discernment so as to see things from the divine perspective, rather than through the prism of our own personal preferences and prejudices.

Inclusive and welcoming

There is a difference between welcoming others into our own communities, and creating a space that is inclusive. Being inclusive can be both liberating and threatening. Jesus included any who came to him, on the assumption that 'whoever is not against us is for us' (Mark 9:40), and in the process included one who would eventually betray him, as well as others whose behaviour gave the religious establishment of the day cause to criticize him (Luke 7:31–34). Today's tribal alliances are emerging because we all have a need to be included in something that is bigger than ourselves. This is more important now than in previous generations, because the culture itself engenders suspicion of strangers – not just of those interlopers in the suburban environment whom we fail to recognize, but even of those whom we see every day, in the workplace or at the school gate. At a time when our inner lives are collapsing, we are creating more and more legal barriers to protect ourselves from others, thereby depriving ourselves of the very networks of support that we actually need if we are to thrive as human beings. This is one of the places where those who follow Jesus ought to be challenging the norms of the culture, because the sort of suspicion that governments now encourage and applaud is actually contrary to the Gospel. Welcoming the stranger is both a social need, and a biblical principle. The great feast to which all are invited (Luke 14:15–24) is a more authentic picture of the Kingdom of God than the sacramental restrictions observed today by churches as diverse as the Roman Catholics and the Plymouth Brethren, strange bedfellows who are united in their regular celebrations of the Eucharist and their insistence on excluding any but their own from it. A central identifying mark of an authentic Gospel community in the twenty-first century (as in the first century) will be hospitality, a gift that invariably blesses those who give as well as those who receive. Christine D. Pohl comments:

> Hospitality will not occur in any significant way in our lives or churches unless we give it deliberate attention. But the practice has been mostly forgotten and because it conflicts with a number of contemporary values, we must intentionally nurture a commitment to hospitality ... Hospitality becomes less difficult and more 'natural' as we grow more familiar with the practice. Grace and gift infuse it in ways that are not easily

accounted for. We experience fulfilment as we give of ourselves, but we can neither explain nor anticipate it.[54]

Ancient and future

Along with this there should be an openness to learn from, and value, the historic tradition as well as more experimental practices that might help to contextualize the Gospel in today's world. Indeed, so far as contextualization is concerned, the two are likely to go hand in hand, for there is a growing awareness in the wider culture that we should not ignore the wisdom of past generations in favour of our own newly minted forms of spiritual expression. Some will be happy with the backward look, because for them any form of contemporary contextualization will always be a bad thing: was not 'the faith' handed on to the saints once and for all? Others will be uneasy with this, believing that each generation should reinvent the Church *ab initio* for itself. The importance of story for today's spiritually lost wayfarers has already been noted in this chapter, and is a theme picked up in much contemporary life. In the novel *Generation X*, Douglas Coupland depicts a group of friends who have withdrawn into the desert to escape the roller-coaster of life and contemplate possible deeper meanings. One of them, Claire,

> breaks the silence by saying that it's not healthy to live life as a succession of isolated little cool moments. 'Either our lives become stories, or there's just no way to get through them.'
> I agree. Dag agrees. We know that this is why the three of us left our lives behind us and came to the desert – to tell stories and to make our own lives worthwhile tales in the process.[55]

This is precisely the way that Jesus operated: inviting people into the bigger story that is the Kingdom of God, while also affirming their own personal stories as having a vital contribution to make to the wholeness of human life. By living within this story, its ancient roots as well as its infinite possibilities, faithful disciples can not only offer hope but can also become an embodiment of a greater future for those whose lives are fragmented and meaningless. Robert Webber has eloquently identified the need for the Church of the future also to be the Church of the past, with his notion of the ancient–future axis of the Gospel.[56] The extent to which any particular Christian community will reflect the historic tradition and its way of doing things will vary with different circumstances, but being faithful to the Christological origins of the Church will never involve a total abandonment of the past. It will, however, require some inspirational leadership from existing church leaders if we are to facilitate the emergence of new forms of spiritual community that might leave behind some of our own most cherished understandings, while at one and the same time adopting ancient practices that some would prefer to relegate to the liturgical scrapheap. The appropriate balance between 'Eschatological preference and Historical Precedence'[57] for the twenty-first century could well push us all into uncharted, and unexpectedly hospitable, waters.

Creating and imagining

Daniel Pink suggests that what we need to help us navigate the threatening waters of the Conceptual Age are 'creators and empathizers, pattern recognizers, and meaning makers ... artists, storytellers, caregivers, consolers, big picture thinkers'.[58] This is another description that, without naming him, could be adopted as an accurate description of Jesus. The sort of spontaneity that is implied by such a statement comes naturally to the sort of people whom Ethan Watters found in the urban tribes that he surveyed, as well as correlating with the research of sociologist Richard Florida into the part played by what he calls the 'creative class' in the regeneration of cultures and cities throughout the world.[59] But creativity is not limited by background, education, or economic status: from a Christian point of view, creativity is the primary attribute of God. It is certainly the first divine attribute to be mentioned in the Bible, and being co-creators with God must therefore constitute a large part of what is meant by the statement that women and men are made in the divine image (Gen. 1:27). A Gospel-centred community will be a space in which the human and divine can meet in creative encounter. One aspect of cultural change that accompanies the reshaping of the urban landscape is the unprecedented growth in places that intentionally create a 'third space'. The online journal *In Third Space* defines this construct as 'a conceptual area that exists beyond conventional categories ... a state of hybridity and fluidity'.[60] More prosaically, Starbucks, the coffee shop chain, has applied this terminology to its own stores, promoting them as a third-space experience where people can spend time creating and enjoying a new community that is somewhere between work (where relationships are generally highly structured and McDonaldized) and home (where isolation and boredom are often the norm). Their introduction of coffee cups bearing wise sayings under the banner of 'the way I see it' serves to underline the ever-present search for meaning and purpose in life by offering customers something to talk about that will lift their conversations beyond the mundane and everyday. Starbucks describe this as 'a way to promote open, respectful conversation among a wide variety of individuals'.[61] When I first came across these cups, and engaged in precisely that sort of conversation over coffee with others who happened to be there, I instantly thought to myself, 'But isn't this what church is supposed to be like?' – or, maybe with greater theological accuracy, 'Isn't this actually church, but it's happening outside the boundaries of what we think church is?' Christians who want to make a difference will be a part of the third spaces of the culture, either by operating within such spaces where they already exist (typically city centres and rural locations), or by helping to create them where there is no common meeting ground for lonely people to find community (typically the suburbs). Jesus knew how to occupy the third spaces of his culture, and always operated in a setting where he would naturally bump into people. That is where discipleship was nurtured and the lost were invited to be a part of the conversation. Without this kind of space, it is hard to follow the apostolic injunctions to build one another up in faith. The inherited paradigm has given us structures that model Sunday services, but few third spaces that can model discipleship.

In the musical *Chicago* there is a song called 'Mr Cellophane'. It is the cry of a man who feels that no one notices him: he might as well be invisible, as if his existence is of no consequence to anyone. A refrain running through the song says:

Mr Cellophane shoulda been my name, Mr Cellophane,
'Cause you can look right through me, walk right by me and never know I'm there. . .

And the song ends with the plaintive cry: 'Hope I didn't take up too much of your time.'

Mr Cellophane speaks for millions of lonely, lost, and hurting souls in today's world who feel that they are invisible and inconsequential to anyone else. Sharon Daloz Parks comments, 'As human beings we all have a need to be "seen" '[62] – but more than that, as people crafted according to the *imago Dei* we all deserve to be valued, not just for our own sake but for God's sake. Somewhere in all that is a clue to what a Gospel community might be like.

3 MISSION

Along with many other traditional terms, the word 'mission' is having a hard time today, and I have often been asked why I continue to use it. For some people it conjures up too many images of imperialism, coercion, aggression, and all the negative aspects of the expansion of Christendom. There is no denying that this has sometimes been the way that Christians have pursued the mission of the Church, whether through the forcible 'conversion' of other peoples at the point of a sword or the more domesticated, but no less abusive, appeals of evangelists who intentionally use psychologically manipulative techniques to persuade their hearers to make 'decisions for Christ'. As if that wasn't enough, Stephen Cottrell reminds us that 'mission' is not a biblical word, and encourages us to speak instead of what God does.[1] In spite of all that, I am (for now anyway) still content to speak of Christians as being people with a mission. The word itself has a much wider currency than its use within the Church, and can be a convenient shorthand way of describing the overarching purposes and values of many different kinds of organizations, including communities of faith. Admittedly, many so-called 'mission statements' are so bland as to be meaningless (including those of many churches), but that should be an invitation to create an understanding that will be empowering and compassionate, rather than abandoning the term altogether. When Christians allow their own traditional language to be hijacked by narrowly defined interest groups, they do no service either to themselves or, ultimately, to the Gospel.

Some personal history

My personal introduction to missiology started in the mid 1980s, when I was invited to become mission convener of the Scottish Churches Council, an organization that at the time was the official ecumenical body of the Scottish churches, founded by the various

Protestant denominations but with involvement of Roman Catholics at both local and national levels.[2] At the time I was a relatively young, completely unknown academic teaching Religious Studies in the University of Stirling, and I have often wondered why I was invited to take on that role, and why I agreed to do it. I know the answer to the second question: the person who invited me was a theology professor in another university, and a highly respected figure in Scottish life, and I reckoned that such an invitation to someone like me was so unexpected that quite possibly God might have something to do with it. Subsequent events tended to confirm my initial assessment, but a lot was to happen before I appreciated that. I doubt that any of the original members of that committee would disagree with me if I say that it was somewhat moribund at the time – like lots of other church committees, this group had an illustrious history and a lot of potential, but seemed to have lost its way somewhat. After my first few meetings, I distinctly remember thinking that I either needed to close it down with as much dignity as possible, or reinvent it so as to connect with the real issues facing the churches in mission at the end of the twentieth century. But first I had my own challenges to face, as it was already dawning on me that I myself knew next to nothing about mission. The way in which I learned is worth recalling in some detail, because it underlines some of the key features that should inform all our missional activity. In the 1980s the UK government had initiated a nationwide movement to revitalize and restore derelict industrial land through the concept of a 'garden festival', and several major cities had their own version, not least because funding was made available for the purpose. The idea was to clean up polluted sites by creating a large parkland area, adding some of the features of a theme park (rides and entertainment), then running the place for a summer season on a commercial basis, after which the theme park elements would be dismantled and the landscaped and revitalized ground returned to the community. One of these events was planned for the city of Glasgow in 1988, and a couple of years prior to that I found myself being invited to a presentation by the organizers, who encouraged us to use it as a showcase for any product that we might wish to bring to the attention of the public during that year. The churches were quick to see the possibilities of this, and one of the first sites to be up and running was a churches pavilion which became a focus for prayer and worship throughout the months that the Glasgow Garden Festival was operational (March to October, as I recall). It was therefore natural for my committee to wonder if there might be some missional initiative that we might contribute to that more extensive Christian presence. It so happened that one member of that group was also General Secretary of the Bible Society, and suggested we designate 1988 as the Scottish Year of the Bible.

That was how I found myself one autumn day in 1986, along with my wife, meeting with the chief executive of the company that was to run this enterprise. It was memorable for several reasons, not least the fact that we drove through such torrential rain to get there that by the time we were picking our way to the temporary building that was his office, the entire site was a sea of mud. Inside, the office itself was enveloped in a thick fog of tobacco smoke, the executive being a chain-smoker and this being before the days when such behaviour was banned in public spaces. I was not altogether sure what it was that we might be asking for, but tentatively suggested that there might be a corner somewhere for the churches to celebrate this particular project on the Bible. I should have been ready for the next question, which was (predictably) an enquiry as to why anyone might still be the slightest bit interested in the Bible, and more especially why people who were paying for a day out should have it thrust upon them by eager Christians. It was a fair question, and the answer evidently turned out to be satisfactory because the conversation then turned to finding a suitable date. Easter was not a possibility because the programme for that day was already organized, and as we thought of other Christian festivals that fell within the time-frame during which the Garden Festival would be operational, Pentecost was the next most obvious one. The company executive had never heard of this, and was intrigued to hear the story from the New Testament book of Acts, of the events of the first Pentecost (Acts 2:1–42). He sat back in his chair, lit more cigarettes, and just as I was fearing that he was going to send us away empty-handed, he commented that this could be a theme worth celebrating in more than just a corner – and offered us the entire 120-acre site for the day, along with a budget big enough to provide a programme for every entertainment spot in the place. With the sort of confidence that is the product either of crass stupidity or of divine insight, I assured him that we could deliver this with no problem at all. I remember driving home wondering what I had done, and more especially how I was going to break this news to my committee. We wanted to be missional, but to do it more or less unobtrusively – and this was way bigger than anything any of us had ever dreamed about! To my surprise, the committee loved it, not least because someone else was going to fund the whole venture. But there was just the small matter of what we might do. For every day that the Garden Festival was open to visitors, they needed 140 programme hours, and we were going to have to provide this in a form that was identifiably Christian while being accessible and acceptable to the general population. The fact that people were paying to get in meant we had to come up with something a bit more engaging than traditional church fare, not least because this was going to take place on a Sunday, and by definition anyone who spent that day at the Garden Festival would have chosen (whether consciously or not) not to be in church. By the time of the Festival, though, we had more than 70 individuals and groups using arts media of every conceivable kind at more than 20 separate locations throughout the 120-acre site, and providing the full 140 hours of programme time – not to mention a worship celebration in a central arena in mid-afternoon. In all, more than 47,000 people streamed through the gates on that day, making it the biggest single attendance for the entire season that the Garden Festival was open, something that was subsequently recognized by an award to my committee from the UK government.

Much of what I think I know about mission has its roots in that experience. It taught me that the *missio Dei* is not just a fancy theological construct, but it is really true. God actually is at work in the world, even in what to Christians can look like a pretty inhospitable environment. More than that, it was a business executive who was a self-proclaimed unbeliever who drew this to my attention by suggesting that if the Gospel really is as important as we say, and if God is truly at work, then we needed to think on the grand scale. I also realized that the sort of paranoia that church people can have about engaging with the wider culture is actually a self-induced fear of stepping out into the public arena as Christians. Others are nothing like as anti-Christian as we can sometimes imagine them to be. But – and this is an important point – I only came to that realization because I was prepared to *listen* to what was going on in a cultural context that in many ways was quite alien to any of my previous experience. It was only on reflecting back afterwards that I realized that I had followed the advice given by Jesus when he sent out the disciples: to go two-by-two with the good news, to wait to be invited in before sharing it, and then to bring blessing into the lives of those who were open (Luke 10:1–12). I was also forced to do some hard thinking about what the Gospel might actually look like in such a space. I already knew in theory that though the Gospel is the same in all times and places (because God is the same), the ways in which it can be contextualized will be diverse and will involve a lot more than just using the culture as a peg on which to hang the message of the Church. But working that out in practical terms called for more creative imagination. I like Martyn Percy's memorable phrase, as he reminds us that 'the lesson from Pentecost is that theology (or Christianity) is always spoken in tongues, so that each can understand in their own language'.[3] In this case, the language had to be embodied in the arts. This was something else I learned out of that experience, because it also became apparent to me that the churches have far more talent and enthusiasm than we sometimes give ourselves credit for. But Christians with the talents that are important for this sort of mission sometimes find themselves marginalized in their local congregations, because what they can do does not always fit into the regular patterns of Sunday worship. As such people were recruited, my wife (who by now was already exploring the value of clowning in ministry) found herself spending a lot of time counselling people with enormous talents, but who felt rejected or misunderstood by their churches.[4] When we listen attentively to the questions of the culture, it is likely to present fresh challenges to our inherited ways of being church alongside the new possibilities for journeying with others who may never otherwise hear the Gospel. I also discovered that mission is better done ecumenically, if only because the wider culture has no understanding of the reasons for the Church's fragmentation and is likely to be far more receptive to an initiative that can genuinely claim to be 'Christian' in the broadest sense of the word. Finally, and to my surprise, I learned that it is possible to move church bureaucracies to change traditional ways of doing things – providing that what is proposed is adventurous and creative, and centred on mission. Pentecost Sunday is a traditional day for confirmations, but the Roman Catholic archbishop of Glasgow adjusted the time for that so he and his flock could be part of the event. Similarly, in the year in question, Pentecost Sunday turned out to be in the week when the General Assembly of the Church of Scotland was meeting in Edinburgh – and coaches were laid on to transport people from one city to the other. Other denominations made similar adjustments to their usual patterns of worship. It would be hard to over-emphasize the impact that experience has had on my own ministry. It has informed my understanding of what mission might look like in a post-modern culture, and engendered my optimism in relation to the impact that traditional churches might have if only they can move forward in creative ways in sharing the good news of the Gospel with those who as yet do not know Christ. It also marked the point at which I started to find myself marginalized within the community of academic theology, which tends to operate on a very narrow definition of what is acceptable, and being a practitioner as well as a theoretician (especially if you are seen to be successful at it) puts you in a fragile position in British academic circles. Even those who advertise their credentials as 'evangelicals' tend to see the evangel as something to be dissected and analysed – and certainly not to be taken beyond the confines of church buildings.

Starting points

In spite of advice from well-meaning friends who advised me to keep such activities separate from my academic interests if I wanted to have any academic career prospects, I was already too far along the road of reflecting and writing about cultural change and contextualization. That event also had a profound effect on my wife's ministry, and what I want to do in the rest of this chapter is to weave together some threads that the two of us have laid out in recent books. Trying to enunciate a grand theory of everything will always be fraught with difficulty, and I expect the connections I make here will not be the last word on the topic, though enough people have become excited about them when the two of us have spoken at conferences along these lines that I know there must be one or two formative ideas in here. The books that are feeding into this are my wife's book, *Spirituality to Go* and my own two volumes, *The McDonaldization of the Church* and *Do Christians Know How to Be Spiritual?*[5] These books were not intentionally written so as to form a series, though it was inevitable that some of the same themes would emerge, if only because they are the things that we both feel passionate about. But it was when people in workshops and seminars started asking how the three books might be connected that I started to reflect on a possible answer to that question. As I did so, I identified three particular strands that might be woven together to form a new understanding of the missional possibilities opening before the Church today. In the first one to be written, *The McDonaldization of the Church*, I identified seven people groups that I suggested might offer a helpful framework within which to think about mission: the desperate poor, hedonists, traditionalists, spiritual searchers, corporate achievers, secularists, and the apathetic. In *Do Christians Know How to Be Spiritual?* I proposed a spectrum identifying three main ways in which the terms 'spiritual' and 'spirituality' are being used in the wider culture – lifestyle, discipline, and enthusiasm – and adopted that as a way of identifying some challenges faced by those who wish to make connections between Christian faith and the search for spiritual meaning that now seems to be endemic in Western society. The sub-title of *Spirituality to Go* is 'rituals and reflections for everyday life', and the book offers a series of ways in which ordinary things that we all do every day might become a focus for intentional spiritual reflection and practice. As I thought about these concepts, I began to wonder if they might be connected, and in the process it occurred to me that not only is there a set of possible connections, but these connections can be used in reimagining some strategic aspects of mission for the twenty-first century.

Before moving on to explore this in more detail, let me take a detour to comment on the way in which I originally came to articulate those seven people groups. When I was writing *The McDonaldization of the Church*, I spent a lot of time reflecting on the usefulness, or otherwise, of this particular taxonomy. Depending on how I felt on a particular day, the chapter in which it was proposed was either included or consigned to the waste-bin. The reason for my prevarication was that, unlike everything else in the book, I was conscious of the fact that there was absolutely no empirical evidence to support the existence of these groups as discrete entities, still less my notion that they might offer a useful lens through which to reflect on the task of the Church today. The process whereby I identified them was entirely intuitive, based on my reflective hunches about the people I meet, and the struggles they face in life, as well as their aspirations and ambitions for the future. Imagine my surprise, then, when reviewers of that book consistently reported a sense of *déjà-vu* in relation to these categories. For several years now I have used them in workshops and conferences with clergy and others, and no one else has managed to identify an empirical basis for them either, but everyone seems to agree that they are a good fit for today's Western culture, and are consistent with other people's perceptions in a way that I have found to be both encouraging and somewhat unsettling. It reminded me of Friedrich Kekule von

Stradonitz's (1829–96) account of how he identified the shape of the benzene molecule as a result of a dream in which he saw a snake eating its own tail. By taking seriously this non-rational (though not irrational) insight, he was able to go on and demonstrate that benzene must have a ring structure. There are many ways of understanding such experiences. Neurologically, it could be a matter of left-brained (rational) thinking being informed by the harder-to-define creativity of the right hemisphere. Christians would no doubt wish to invoke the work of the divine Spirit who 'will teach you everything' (John 14:26) by suggesting ideas that we may not otherwise have thought about. Others may want to argue that asking this sort of rational cause-and-effect question just shows that we are out of touch with the way the cosmos really is, and we would do better to accept that all things – wisdom included – are interconnected in ways we shall never fully comprehend.

Whatever the explanation, the realization has dawned on me in recent years that what we have been taught to think of as 'mere' intuitions are likely to be as valuable as opinions that can be spelled out on the basis of empirical research and well-grounded evidence – or, rather, that intuition can be valid empirical evidence.[6] It seems to me that effective Christian mission in today's world is going to be like that – more intuitive than rational, and depending more on relational and interpersonal skills than on neatly ordered and logical presentations of Christian doctrine. That is not to say that I wish to either ditch or distance myself from the classic creeds of the Church, nor indeed from intellectual reflection on the faith, but rather that I doubt whether rational argument is now the most appropriate way in which to commend the Gospel within the context of today's postmodern culture. What follows here, then, is – depending on one's point of view – either so speculative as to be worthless, or based on that intuitive wisdom which Richard Florida associates with the creative classes,[7] and which the New Testament might describe as the work of the Spirit.

Understanding people

Before exploring this in greater detail, I will need to reiterate and summarize these previous ideas for the benefit of readers who are not familiar with them already. Those who have read the previous books should also be reassured that I have not just done a cut-and-paste job here, but have summarized my ideas anew and in the process added some fresh insights and made some modifications to what I have previously suggested.

My initial starting point for this way of looking at the Church and the culture was a sense that much of the Church's problems seem to stem from the fact that, to a large extent, the ways of being church that we now have match the concerns of only a certain kind of person, at a time when the culture is more openly diverse than it has ever been. In recent years, we in the Global North have become more aware of the ethnic diversity of the world – and, in the process, have become increasingly paranoid about the possibility of different peoples being able to live together in harmony. The question of what a globalized Christianity might look like is a major issue within that frame of reference, as also is the question of how Christians might relate meaningfully to people of other world faiths. These are not, however, the questions with which I am concerned here. But the uncertainty about these matters is both a cause and a symptom of a more widespread crisis in Western identity that is reshaping the way people live their lives, and therefore the way they relate to others, in matters of faith as in all other aspects of life. It is only people who are comfortable with their own identity who know how to relate meaningfully to others. There are many useful ways of reflecting on our own identity, and some of them (such as psychological personality types or ethnicity) are capable of traditional empirical exploration. The concept of socially determined people groups is less precise than that, but I believe no less useful in relation to the missional possibilities with which Christians are now presented.

The notion that there might be specific people groups in the culture, each with their own challenges and opportunities (and, therefore, ways of relating to whatever it is that may help them to find identity and purpose in life), is nothing new. In the past they would have tended to be identified by reference to factors such as age or inherited social standing, or other prescribed socio-economic factors. This way of looking at people still has validity, and much church life is organized on this basis, with groups for children, young parents, singles, older people, women, men, and so on. The terminology now being used to describe such groupings might be new (Gen X, Gen Y, builders, boomers, busters), but the reality is the same, and most Christians who think of culture tend to be attracted to generationally based categories of understanding. This is no longer the whole picture, and may not in fact be the most useful part of the picture in relation to mission. For there is another way of looking at people groups, which emerges from neither biologically nor culturally determined norms, but is a natural outcome of the fragmented nature of contemporary Western culture, which both encourages and enables the choice of self-invented 'liquid identities'. Advertisers come up with slick slogans such as '50 is the new 40' (and its equivalents for other age groups), and while that may not necessarily be an accurate description in the case of any given individual, it is a way of acknowledging that identity today is not some fixed construct that is determined by external forces, but something that we choose for ourselves, or which comes pre-packaged, as it were, with other lifestyle choices that we may consciously make.

Our lengthening life-spans certainly contribute to this, as one simple example will illustrate. In the past, a long marriage would have been 25 years (hence the marking of that as a 'silver anniversary'), with 40 years being attained by a much smaller number, and 50 being an anniversary that – if it was achieved at all – was likely to come only at the very end of life, while anything longer than that was certainly regarded as exceptional. Moreover, sexual activity would have been confined to the first ten or fifteen years of marriage, after which a relationship would typically have settled down into a comfortable companionship 'until death us do part'. Many factors have conspired to change all those things. Our expectations of sexual fulfilment have been transformed, not only by medical advances in conception and contraception, but also by the openness with which such topics are now addressed, which means that the average person today knows far more about these things than previous generations, and we have an expectation that older age and sexual activity are not mutually exclusive categories and that relationships should be fulfilling physically, mentally, and spiritually at every stage of life. Things have changed radically and rapidly in the last 40 years, and even our own grandparents would be amazed at the shape of relationships today. Historically, the family was primarily an economic unit, and our forebears had children in order to secure the economic future, of themselves as well as of the wider family and community, and ultimately the nation. The idea that a relationship might itself be a source of personal growth and nurture was either unknown, or was regarded as an unexpected bonus if and when it happened. It was unheard of for individuals who had been married for 30 or 40 years to split up in order to find a better quality of relationship, yet that is now increasingly commonplace, and in

Britain a growing sector of the clubbing scene (which until quite recently would have been regarded as the exclusive preserve of people in their twenties and thirties) focuses on the niche market of over-fifties who are looking to find new partners. Part of the explanation for this is the simple fact that in the past, over-fifties would have felt they had little to look forward to, and even Erik Erikson characterized the over-sixties as 'waiting for death'.[8] In that context, a 'lifetime' relationship might not have lasted much beyond a quarter of a century, so most of our forebears were never faced with the prospect of nurturing intimacy over such a long period of time.

The last of my grandparents died in the late 1970s, but if any of them were to come back today one thing that would certainly surprise them would be the ways in which we now regularly reinvent ourselves, not only conceptually but even physically. The fascination for genealogical research, as people right across the age and social spectrum seek to uncover their ancestors – and the ease with which it can be done, with online census returns that can take us back to the middle of the nineteenth century at the touch of a button – is part of this search for a new identity. Nowadays, we not only scan documentary evidence from the past: we also enlist science in the form of DNA testing to dig back behind the official statements in an effort to understand who we 'really' are. I just put the terms 'DNA ancestry testing' into an internet search engine, and came up with 850,000 sites, of which all the top hits connected me to laboratories where you can send your DNA samples and receive back an analysis of the ethnic mix that has combined to produce the person you are today. By understanding who we think we are, we also believe that we can change who we truly are, and increasing numbers of people do both. When I was a teenager in high school, we all knew that sex change was possible, but only in the same sort of disconnected way that we knew Saturn had rings. No one that I can recall had any direct knowledge of it actually happening. Today, not only is gender realignment a recognized and safe medical procedure, but most of us will either know personally or come across transsexual persons in the course of our everyday life. The massive rise in cosmetic surgery is another indicator of the way in which people who regard themselves as 'ordinary' are taking control of their lives and becoming who they want to be. For every person who takes such drastic measures to live their dream, a multitude of others reinvent themselves in more modest ways in the search for an identity and purpose that will give meaning to life. And if our initial choices fail to work out, then we can always keep on changing till the day we die.

This is the fluid context in which I am thinking of both people groups and the spiritual spectrum. Bearing in mind, then, that we can, and do, consciously and unconsciously shift from one people group to another, let us briefly reflect on the groups I originally identified as being significant for the mission of the Church.

My first group are the *desperate poor*, by which I mean people who are either homeless, or very nearly so. Many factors have conspired to create a situation in which beggars are now regularly seen on the streets of cities in the Global North in a way that would not have been the case 20 years ago. This is not the place to rehearse the reasons for this, though the growing incidence of poverty is undoubtedly one by-product of the increasing McDonaldization of culture, with its accompanying regulation of every conceivable activity in such a way that poor people today are excluded from participation in any form of legal economic activity. The arrival of significant numbers of refugees seeking a safe life in the Global North is adding to the numbers of the desperate poor throughout Europe in particular, not least because (as in Britain) 'the rules' (McDonaldized systems) often prohibit them from engaging in any work that might enable them to escape from poverty. This topic could form the basis of an entire book by itself, and I need to avoid commenting on it further so as to focus on my central question here, namely: what would 'spirituality' look like for someone in this circumstance? And how might the resources of the Christian tradition connect with those concerns in a missional frame of reference?

Hedonists are a second group who can also be easily identified. By this, I mean those people who deal with the discontinuities and pressures of life by partying at every possible opportunity. Anyone who doubts that this happens on any significant scale need only to be in the main streets of any British city at 2 a.m. on a Saturday or Sunday morning, when they can easily be thronging with thousands of people. Some cities become virtual war-zones at this time, and the emergency rooms of our hospitals have their busiest period of the entire day, with violence often erupting there as well. The culture of binge drinking is alarming politicians as well as healthcare workers, as they contemplate what this will mean for future life expectancy and the health of the nation. This way of life is not as obvious in other Western nations as it is in the UK, but the underlying trend is still there – even in the USA, where different notions of what constitutes a public nuisance tend to keep such behaviour off the streets and restricted to private spaces. It is easy to parody and despise this clubbing and party-going lifestyle, but the reality is that growing numbers (of younger people in particular) find that the realities of life are just too painful to deal with head-on, and this is the only way to get through from one day to the next. My wife and I are regulars at a gym not far from where we live, and conversations in the changing rooms can be very revealing. While I have been writing this chapter, we were at the gym early on a Saturday evening, and my wife overheard a conversation with a young woman (a quintessential 'Bridget Jones' type), who commented that, with any good fortune, she would be drunk within an hour of leaving the gym – and planned to stay that way right through the weekend. You might wonder why anyone would spend time and money at the gym trying to keep healthy, while having that aspiration for a good weekend. But that is the sad reality for so many people: life is fragmented and painful, and if it is to continue at all there need to be regular and frequent moments when the pain is obliterated. If that can happen in the presence of other people who provide a sense of community and belonging for a few hours, then so much the better. Of course, not everyone who engages in this sort of hedonistic lifestyle is consciously motivated by such considerations, but the fact that so much contemporary dance music comes with lyrics highlighting loneliness and pain suggests that it is by no means an isolated experience.

Traditionalists are another group, and by this designation I mean people who, it might appear, time has passed by. They would be unlikely to have the sort of lifestyle just described. Quite the reverse: they feel at home with traditional values, whether in personal morality or social structures, and may be somewhat resistant to what they regard as the unhealthy encroachment of post-modern questions, let alone the answers that may be on offer. These are people who feel deeply rooted in their local communities, who wish to preserve a sense of continuity both with their own past and also with the inherited story of their nation, as they understand it. They expect marriages to be forever, and want their children to follow in their footsteps. They are the people who tick a box in a census return to identify themselves as being 'Christian' not because they necessarily have any particular faith commitments, but more as a statement that they do not belong to some other faith community that they regard as alien and intrusive. Though they may think of themselves as tolerant people, others might regard them as racist and xenophobic, accepting diversity just so long as it never impinges on or threatens their own settled way of doing things. It is quite a challenge to find appropriate language with which to describe this group, and I have tried to use the term 'traditionalist' without any implied value judgement. The Gospel will bring a challenge to all the groups identified here, traditionalists included. But that is not the same as saying that they are bad people – any more than I would wish to label the desperate poor or the hedonists, or any of the others, in that way. They are culturally conservative, and represent the kind of oral culture in which, as Walter Ong has noticed, people do not so much live in the past, as use the stories and memories of the past in order to serve the present.[9] It may be tempting to identify these people as blue-collar or working-class individuals, but this is not an economic category as such, and many upwardly mobile and so-called middle-class people are also traditionalists in the sense that they live for their immediate surroundings, rather than concerning themselves with making history or changing the world. As I noted in *The McDonaldization of the Church*, there are detailed differences in traditionalist lifestyles, depending on whether they are urban or rural, just as there are differences between traditional people in different countries. But wherever we look, they are characterized by a love for traditional family values, loyalty to national institutions and to their own friends, and a strong sense of right and wrong, often combined with a fierce independence of spirit.

Spiritual searchers may have just as much pain in their lives as all the other groups, but they handle it in a different way than those mentioned so far. For a variety of reasons, they believe there is some kind of resolution that lies beyond the everyday, and that the establishment of a 'spiritual' connection will be central to that. They may be people from all walks of life, and will also overlap with other groups mentioned here. Some spiritual searchers might also be hedonists, and the drink and drug fuelled culture of the clubbing scene can represent one aspect of a wider search for transcendence. On the other hand, most spiritual searchers will not typically be attracted by that. Though there is no universal profile of this sort of person, they might easily be artistic and intuitive, and in fact have several characteristics in common with the creative class who will be mentioned in a later chapter. In terms of age profile, they cover the whole spectrum, from teenagers to people in their nineties and beyond. In relation to the Church, they are the people who would describe themselves as 'spiritual but not religious'. Some may be anti-Christian, but a significant number of them are likely to have had some sort of connection with the Church, and maintain a high level of respect for the good things that Christians have contributed to the wider culture. Traditional Christians may regard them as anarchic, with their commitment to free speech, their fascination with the heterodox ideas of groups such as the Gnostics, and a tendency to mix-and-match whatever spiritual goodies may seem relevant to their concerns. At the same time, they might well have a more integrated sense of identity and purpose, with every aspect of life being interconnected and little sense of a discontinuity between the secular and the sacred. The searchers have a keen awareness of the disintegration and fragmentation of Western culture, and want to do something about it. Because they see traditional values as part of the problem, they will often find themselves in conflict with those I have labelled 'traditionalists', though they are as likely as them to be bothered about establishing moral norms for themselves and their children, albeit through a self-invented value system rather than unquestioning acceptance of inherited societal norms. Above all, perhaps, the searchers are experimenters: they try things out first, and then reflect on them later. In that sense, they are quintes-sential reflective practitioners, and as such they also demonstrate a considerable overlap with the creative class.

In my earlier book, I described the spiritual searchers as if they constituted one single grouping, whereas in fact there are two dis-crete sub-groups within this category, depending on whether the spiritual resolution is seen as coming from outside one's everyday experience of life here and now, or whether the secret of fulfilment is perceived as a more internally generated quality. Put another way, some spiritual searchers are dualists, while others adopt a more holistic view of things. I have deliberately chosen not to contrast dualists with monists here, as that is not quite an accurate char-acterization of what I wish to highlight. The reasoning behind that distinction will become clear later on in this chapter, when I suggest some ways in which these people groups can be correlated alongside the spectrum of concerns that are now being described as 'spiritual'.

The *corporate achievers* are individuals who, as the term suggests, are focused on making it to the top as high-flyers in whatever pro-fessional sphere they operate in. As such, they are to be found predominantly in big business, though they might also be in academia and healthcare, as those sectors of the economy increasingly abandon collegiate and pastoral structures in favour of managerial solutions. Such people are determined to 'live the dream' by getting to the top, regardless of the possible consequences. In the past, people tended to become leaders in organizations by virtue of long service and experience, which was assumed to equate to knowledge and understanding. Today, such traditional virtues are regarded as quaint and outmoded. Though governments are trying to legislate against ageism, the tendency for older people to be marginalized in the workplace has never been greater. This is partly related to the rampant individualism and selfishness that consumerism has engendered, so that colleagues are no longer partners but are regarded as competitors in the game of career advancement. It is also connected to the fact that individuals who still hanker after a collegiate environment are less inclined to engage in aggressive self-promotion, and will often choose to resign rather than become caught up in battles for personal aggrandizement. This trend is having serious consequences for traditional businesses and institutions, leading to the loss of the wisdom of people with experience, and a consequent lack of appropriate mentoring for others. It is particularly noticeable in education, where older people are being forced out – often, paradoxically, then to reinvent themselves by selling their services back on a freelance basis to the very system that declared them to be unwanted. It is not just an age-related issue, though, as growing numbers of people of all ages are now choosing to down-size their work ambitions in order to spend time with their families, or just to become more human and humane. Much more could be said about that, as it is a trend that affects adversely theological education and training for ministry just as much as it does the work of high schools and universities.

In relation to the theme of this chapter, though, there is one significant pastoral and missional consequence of the scramble for corporate achieving. The simple fact is that the majority of people whom I have labelled 'corporate achievers' are not *achievers* at all, because by definition most of them never make it to the top. Not only do they spend inordinate amounts of time and energy striving to reach an unattainable place, but the experience of feeling constantly undervalued and exploited by one's colleagues in the workplace is one of the major contributing factors to stress and anxiety, leading to misery for the majority and serious mental illness for some. Individuals whose ambitions are entirely focused on corporate achievement generally find that their lives become so dominated by work and their concept of what constitutes appropriate professional standing that they find themselves sacrificing existing relationships, while having no time to nurture new ones. Moreover, even those who make it to the top often find it to be not only a lonely place, but a morally and spiritually disempowering space, especially if they ever pause long enough to reflect on the number of other people they might have destroyed in the process of achieving their own promotions. It is no surprise, then, to find that there is a significant overlap between those who aspire to the corporate dream and the hedonists whose lives are so painful that the only way they can get from one week to the next is through constant partying or over-indulgence in drink and drugs. Corporate achievers can – and do – become spiritual searchers, but most of those who make that transition find that in the process they distance themselves more and more from the lifestyle of the corporate world. Despite the hype of many self-help books and professional training courses, there are very few, if any, who treat 'spirituality' as just another consumer product that will enable them to succeed, and those who start off thinking that way soon end up in the same disillusioned place as so many of their peers, as they find that it fails to deliver on its promises.[10] What would a meaningful and truly empowering Gospel sound like for these people? Some of them will already be connected with churches, and may even be entrusted with positions of influence, though their motivation for such involvement may well be more related to a desire for social acceptance in those places where church connections still have civic currency (which is more likely to be the case in the USA than in Britain or Europe, Canada, Australia, or New Zealand). Most such people are likely to feel miserable and disconnected from their own deepest values, as well as struggling with fragmented relationships – challenges that are not unique to this group, of course, but which certainly occur in exaggerated form among them.

When I wrote *The McDonaldization of the Church*, I dealt with what I called *secularists* in a fairly small paragraph that was largely limited to noting the disproportionate influence that such people have in forming national opinions, especially in the European context. That is still the case. In 2001, for example, the UK census statistics revealed that 72 per cent of people had ticked a box declaring themselves to be 'Christian', while only 16 per cent of people claimed to be 'of no faith'. These returns were of particular significance because, though the actual form of the question varied among the different nations that constituted the United Kingdom, in all parts (England, Scotland, Wales, Northern Ireland) it was a voluntary question.[11] For that reason alone, we can be sure that those respondents who chose to answer it must have felt strongly about *something*. It was a surprise to everyone (including the church leaders) that so many claimed to be 'Christian' and so few claimed to be 'of no faith'. Ever since, there have been arguments as to what any of this might possibly mean – which is a fair enough question, given that only 6.3 per cent of the English population have any regular connection with the Church.[12] Secularists tended to claim that to regard oneself as 'Christian' was more of a default position than anything else, and may even have been a statement that, while having no particular connection to Christianity, the respondents were most definitely not of some other world faith. It therefore became, in effect, a statement about ethnicity or culture and not about faith. No doubt some individuals did indeed intend to make that sort of statement, but it strains credibility to imagine that this could have motivated three quarters of the population. Supposing that explanation was good for even a half of that number, it would still leave a very substantial group of people whose response might be understood to indicate that, at the very least, they are not hostile to Christian values, and may even positively embrace them. In recent years, some British Christians have worked themselves into a paranoid frenzy of believing that the entire culture is against them. That idea is clearly questionable, and the challenge in relation to mission is how to connect with the spiritual concerns of people who either think they are 'secular' or who would be regarded as such by social analysts.

In relation to our theme here, the notion of what it means to be 'secular' is itself questionable. On the one hand there is much evidence that the traditional secularization thesis no longer matches all the facts, and as a result it is being either abandoned or substantially modified by the social science fraternity. In addition, though, there is the growing trend for 'secular' people to concern themselves with 'spiritual' matters and to complain that religious people have robbed the term of meaning for others who do not share their belief structures. In an article on this subject, scientist Michael Shermer begins by affirming, 'I am an atheist', and later gives his definition of what, for him, would constitute 'spirituality':

Spirituality is a way of being in the world, a sense of one's place in the cosmos, a relationship to that which extends beyond ourselves.[13]

Richard Dawkins, well known for his aggressively atheistic attitude through the best-selling book, *The God Delusion*,[14] is on record as making similarly ambiguous statements. In an interview with Ruth Gledhill, religion correspondent of *The Times* newspaper, he recommended that children should be taught the Bible, and confessed not only that he has a soft spot for the Church of England, but also believes that there is more to life – and the universe – than we presently know. In this interview, he talks about 'something wonderful and amazing and something difficult to understand' in light of which 'all theological conceptions will be seen as parochial and petty by comparison'.[15] A search for topics like 'atheist spirituality' or 'secular spirituality' on the internet will also reveal some surprises, coming up with thousands of websites. Some are undoubtedly more significant than others in relation to Christian mission, but when there is even one entitled 'Atheists for Jesus',[16] then surely we ought to take note of a trend that I believe to be as significant as it is unexpected. On the other hand, why should we be surprised by this? A significant amount of neurological and psychological research is highlighting something that Augustine acknowledged centuries ago, that 'You have made us for yourself, O God, and our hearts are restless till they rest in you.'[17] Again, this is not a wholly self-contained category: by definition, some secularists will be hedonists and corporate achievers and, as I have just indicated, some of them might even be included (at least by their own definitions) among the spiritual searchers.

My final people group is *the apathetic*. I suspect that a majority of the people who ticked the 'Christian' box in the 2001 UK census probably fall into this category. They are 'Christians' by default because they are too apathetic to take initiatives to reflect on anything to do with faith, and so they go through life in this – as in other respects – simply following what they have imbibed from their childhood. These people have no aspiration other than to get through from one day to the next with as little disruption or exertion as possible. Some of them may be cynical, and end up among the ranks of the apathetic because of bad experiences. There could be some overlap with corporate achievers, in particular with those who have been so disempowered by being devalued in the workplace that they simply give up on ambition and vision and internalize their cynicism about systems and people in ways that then distance them from active engagement with just about anything other than coping with the immediate moment. In terms of possible connections with church life, my category of the apathetic probably has a fair degree of overlap with those whom others would call 'nominal' Christians – that is, people who wish to be identified with the organization, but with no discernibly significant level of commitment.[18] Some traditionalists may fall into this category, as also may some of the desperate poor, though hedonists, spiritual searchers and secularists are unlikely also to be apathetic, if only because effort and intentionality are key driving forces among those groups.

The spiritual spectrum

In *Do Christians Know How to Be Spiritual?* I proposed a spectrum covering the various ways in which the terms 'spiritual' and 'spirituality' seem now to be used in everyday speech. For a detailed explanation of how I arrived at this idea, I will have to refer readers to that book. In brief, I identified a spectrum with various gradations on it but with three major points, which I named Lifestyle, Discipline, and Enthusiasm. The chief characteristics of these can best be illustrated diagrammatically, as follows:

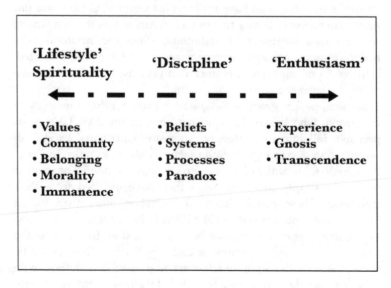

For some people, a 'spiritual experience' can be as apparently ordinary as a meal with friends and family, wholesome food, fine wine, and good conversation – or, for that matter, any number of other 'everyday' experiences and situations that are uplifting and satisfying. That is what I mean by 'lifestyle spirituality'. It is a growing phenomenon and, as I shall suggest below, has major significance in relation to meaningful Christian mission. Other people would not necessarily discount the value of what I have just described, but would only regard something as 'spiritual' if it has a clear connection with the structures of a given belief system, underwritten by a coherent worldview that will quite possibly be expressed through propositional statements, whether Christian or of some other faith. Finally, there is a third group, who would not necessarily question or reject these other two understandings, but for whom nothing meaningfully 'spiritual' could ever happen without some direct encounter with the transcendent, whether through receiving messages from aliens or angels, or speaking in tongues, or some other mystical or ecstatic experience that goes beyond the expected norms of everyday life. I imagine that most readers of this book will have encountered all three sections of this spectrum at some time and, if you are like me, you will perhaps be able to recall different episodes of your own life that connect with one or other of them. Just as with my taxonomy of people groups, so these three aspects of the spiritual do not exist in hermetically sealed compartments without any connection from one to the other. That is why in this diagram I have included the broken arrows along the top, to indicate some sense of interconnection and interplay, connections to which we will now turn our further attention in asking how this spectrum of the spiritual relates to the various types of people discussed earlier, and how both these things connect to the mission of the Church. Here is another diagram that may help to unpack the answer to those questions:

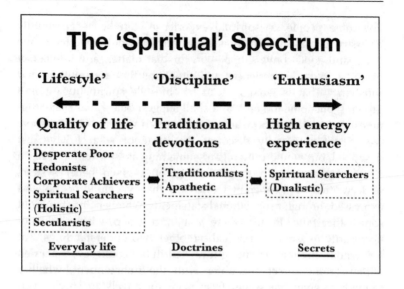

No one will quarrel with the assertion that the most important issue for the desperate poor will be lifestyle and quality of life. Without the basic necessities of life, nothing else is possible. This was the conclusion of Abraham Maslow in his study of the lives of car workers in Detroit, carried out in the 1960s. On this basis he constructed his famous hierarchy of needs, which depicted the meaningful human life ascending through the possession of food, shelter, and health, to experiences of safety and security, as a necessary basis for the nurturing of companionship and sharing of affection, which in turn he believed to be an essential foundation for self-esteem and the ability to value others. Finally, at the top of his hierarchy (often depicted diagrammatically as a triangle) he placed 'self-actualization'.[19] It was in this somewhat rarefied environment that he located his definition of 'spirituality'. In other words, he concluded that exploring what he regarded as the spiritual was something to which people turned only once their other, more basic needs in life had been met. Since most people spend most of their life struggling with the challenge of personal identity and meaningful relationships, this led to the conclusion that spirituality would inevitably be a minority interest. In reality, that has never been the case, not least because the world's poorest people have very often been among the most spiritually engaged. In terms of lifestyle, one only has to mix with people living on the streets to see that, for they look out for each other and care for each other in ways that often put to shame the attitudes of other, better-off sections of the community. One of the cities with which I am most familiar is Santa Barbara in California, where there is a substantial population of people living on the streets, many of them people of great creativity and energy, and not a little education, who enjoy a lifestyle of support and mutuality that, in Christian terms, reflects much that the Church is supposed to embody. But it is not just the desperate poor for whom daily lifestyle is the entry point into the spiritual. The hedonists and corporate achievers are unlikely to be economically poor, but their inner heart may be more empty than that of those who seem to have nothing. I have already described the stress and anxiety that is everyday life for such people, and if they are to find healing and new direction, then everyday life is where it will begin. The same thing is true for holistic spiritual searchers, but for different reasons, this time focused around concerns about the environment, sustainability, meaningful personal relationships, and so on. Secularists, likewise, tend to be bothered about such things. These groups are unlikely to place a high priority on traditional belief systems, either because the need to survive is all-consuming (as it is for the desperate poor, the hedonists, and corporate achievers) or because traditional religious ways are perceived to be contributing factors to the state the world is now in (a commonly held view among spiritual searchers and secularists).

Traditional people, along with the apathetic, are likely to regard all this as too woolly and diffuse for their liking, preferring to locate spiritual meaning in something more tangible and rational such as belief systems and structured ways of thinking. Though Christians bemoan what they see as the churches' failure to connect with the emerging culture of the twenty-first century, they are not generally as ineffective as Christians think. The reality is that traditional churches connect with people who operate in this kind of way. The success of Alpha and similar courses is due to the fact that there is still a substantial number of people who are looking for a spiritual 'theory of everything' and for whom anything 'spiritual' needs to have a rational core of disciplined thinking. I do not mean to suggest that other types of people do not think, or that those who prefer their spirituality to come pre-packaged in this way are not concerned about lifestyle. It is about entry points, something that I will explain more expansively below. One of the unexpected media stories of recent years has been the popularity of two TV series produced by the BBC, *The Monastery* and *The Convent* (and subsequently copied on American TV). In these programmes, groups of volunteers went to live, respectively, in a monastery and a convent to see how or if the experience could affect their lives. At first glance, it might seem as if these programmes contradict my claim here, for the individuals who took part in them fell squarely into the categories of hedonists, corporate achievers, spiritual searchers, and secularists. It is certainly difficult to think of anything more disciplined than this kind of cloistered life. But the interesting thing is that the individuals who found this experience meaningful were, virtually without exception, attracted by aspects of the lifestyle rather than the underlying belief system. In other words, on my definitions, it was questions of how to live, rather than questions about what to believe, that were the most significant.

Finally, those who define the spiritual by reference to high-energy experiences tend to be limited to the category of dualistic spiritual searchers. These are people who may seek out experiences of angels, who may channel messages from extraterrestrials, or who believe implicitly in the power of clairvoyance, runes, or ancient rituals of one sort or another, often involving mystical healing or out-of-body experiences. They tend to grab the headlines, if only because their approach is so radically different from the experience of most people. The reality is, however, that they constitute a tiny minority even within that spectrum of individuals who would describe themselves as spiritually curious.[20] There have always been peaks of such interest, and in terms of today's spiritual spectrum the last peak of this type was in the 1980s and early 1990s, typified by the experiences of people like Hollywood actress Shirley Maclaine who turned her own story of such encounters into several books and a TV miniseries.[21] There are no statistics that I am aware of, but all my observations of the spiritual matrix of the twenty-first century tell me that this sort of interest, while still there (as it always has been throughout history), is not now at the cutting edge of the spiritual search.

Spirituality, mission, and ways of being church

So how does all this relate to the Church's mission? In making the connection, I want first of all to make some observations about cultural change and the dominance of different styles of church, before offering some suggestions as to how the Gospel might best be presented in this ever-evolving scene. Here is another diagram that will serve as a useful starting point:

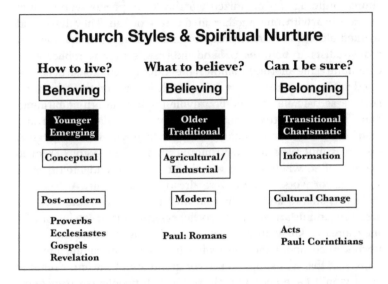

The first thing to say about this is that it would be better as a three-dimensional diagram, but in this medium we have to live within the limitations of the printed page. My proposal is simple enough, though, and can be summarized as follows. Might it be that these different aspects of the 'spiritual' are reflected in different ways of being church, and that these in turn reflect the different cultural contexts in which they came to birth? It is not hard to connect the 'disciplined thinking' style of spirituality with traditional church, which of course had its origins in cultural circumstances that themselves depended on structural discipline: in the case of the Catholic tradition (in its various forms) that was the feudal world of the Agricultural Age, while the Free Church denominations took their shape from the rather different style of discipline of the Industrial Age. In their present form, both traditions have been filtered through the sieve of modernity, which had the effect of prioritizing the cerebral and cognitive aspects of traditional church. There is something else here, though, which will highlight the inadequacy of trying to think of all this in a one-dimensional mode. No matter which sector of the ecclesiastical tradition we look at, our forms of worship and ways of being church have all been inherited from a world and way of being that was very different from what we know today. Whether influenced by the Agricultural Age or its industrial counterpart, the people who historically gathered in church buildings for organized worship were people who were in relationship with one another in the rest of life. They lived and worked alongside each other, and it is no coincidence that the first industrialists, in both the UK and the USA, sought to replicate the community life of rural communities through the construction of 'model villages' and, in some cases, whole towns, some of which still survive as discrete entities. Bournville (now a suburb of Birmingham, but still centred on the Cadbury's chocolate factory) and Hershey, Pennsylvania (another chocolate town) would be good examples, but they are by no means unique. The point I want to make is that, when people who lived, worked, and intermarried gathered for worship, they were already a community, whose lifestyle was shared and interwoven Monday through Saturday, and worship (and its accompanying belief system) was a blessing of who they already knew themselves to be. It was not that they were unconcerned about the spirituality of what I am calling lifestyle, more that this was simply taken for granted. But the entry point to what would have been thought of by such people as distinctively 'spiritual' came through encounter with the worldview and belief systems that enabled them to make sense of how they naturally lived.

I have mentioned the notion of an entry point more than once already, and this is central to what I am thinking here. It explains why I have identified this inherited, traditional form of church with the people I call traditionalists and the apathetic. It is not that these individuals are not concerned about their faith having a practical expression in lifestyle, but rather that they have an assumed and settled shape of lifestyle that is taken for granted, and certainly is not a source of anxiety for them in the way it is for other groups. Moreover, by distinguishing this style of church from what I have called the 'transitional charismatic', with its emphasis on direct mystical experience,[22] I do not mean to imply that people in a traditional church have no interest in personal experience of the divine. But the entry point into spiritual reality for traditional people is unlikely to be, in the first instance, questions about either experience or lifestyle. I see the same overlaps and interchangeability between the concerns of the other two groups I have identified here. There are undoubtedly those (dualist spiritual searchers) whose main entry point into the Church is likely to be through the sort of church that lays emphasis on spiritual gifts, healings, speaking in tongues, and other mystical manifestations. That is not to imply that charismatic Christians have no belief systems, or that lifestyle issues are not significant in such a context. The same with the lifestyle entry point, which I identify especially with today's post-modern generation and, in ecclesiastical terms, with the emerging church. It is not that emerging churches have no beliefs, or that they will necessarily marginalize experience (though they do typically define spiritual experience in a different way than charismatics might). Rather, that lifestyle is the entry point into further exploration of and reflection on the Gospel.

In the diagram, I have included the familiar trio of 'Believing – Belonging – Behaving' as a further way of thinking about this. The inherited structure of church places them in that order, and (with variations on the theme) all churches have traditionally insisted that belief comes first, followed by belonging (that is, acceptance as part of the community of Christ's disciples), and behaviour in a way reflective of the Gospel is the final stage, which may actually take a lifetime and more to perfect. It has become commonplace in recent years to question that pattern, on the basis that belonging is likely to be the first step on the road to Christian discipleship, and that Christians need to learn how to journey alongside others rather than attempting to persuade them of the truth of Christian belief systems and doctrines. I have myself used that terminology of belonging before believing, and still regard it is an appropriate way of expressing how many people will come to faith. It is not, however, the whole picture, and in the light of current concerns for a spirituality that will encompass the whole of life, may not be the most important part of the picture. It is not coincidental that more of my people groups seem to fit into the 'lifestyle' end of the spiritual spectrum than anywhere else, for that is where personal alienation and fragmentation are most acutely experienced, and consequently where healing will need to begin.

I have also included on the diagram a section identifying certain parts of the Scriptures which I believe connect most effectively with these diverse entry points into spiritual exploration. They speak for themselves, though I need to add that the books indicated here are far from exhaustive and could (and should) be expanded and added to – but there is only so much that can be squeezed into a single diagram before it becomes too cluttered. Readers will not be surprised to learn that in seminars I have regularly been asked whether this means that I want to ditch chunks of the Bible, or indeed of the wider Christian tradition. The answer to that is no. An image to help explain my thinking would be that of a traditional jazz band. Who is the leader in a jazz band? Those who know anything about jazz will recognize that as being a very silly question. The nature of the music requires that, at any given moment, the trumpeter might be the leader, then the saxophonist, followed maybe by the vocalist, pianist, bass player, or whoever. At the same time, they all need to be playing in the background in order to provide the infrastructure that gives meaning to the role of the lead instrument. I have come to think of the Christian tradition in that way. At particular historical moments, different aspects of Scripture, and of the wider tradition, have been pre-eminent, and their pre-eminence has been determined by their ability to speak into the cultural needs of the moment. In the earliest centuries of the Church, the main image used of Jesus was that of the Good Shepherd. Why? Well, in times of persecution, that spoke to the hearts of suffering people. They needed safety and security, and the Good Shepherd was the one who would provide it. Jesus was still, of course, Christ, Lord, Saviour, and a plethora of other images familiar from the New Testament, but they were not the terms that spoke to the need of that moment. They were the instruments playing in the background, but were not at that point leading from centre stage. If we move forward to the time of the Reformation, we can see a similar phenomenon. St Paul's letter to the Romans had been in the Bible for 1500 years before Martin Luther 'discovered' it, but it was the circumstances of his day, and his own questions about guilt, that enabled new questions to be addressed to it, and liberated it to move out of the shadows into a prominent place. A similar pattern can be traced in every historical period. In fact, it reflects the way the New Testament itself was written. Why else do we have four Gospels, and not one, except that different nuances and metaphors spoke more profoundly to different cultural and spiritual contexts within the ancient world itself? To address the lifestyle questions of today's people, we will need to engage in the hermeneutical equivalent of improvisation by dusting off some parts of the Bible that have been neglected in the past, for they do indeed have wisdom for our time.

Weaving the threads

I began this chapter by warning readers that my conclusions would be difficult to justify by reference to empirical investigation or rational reflection. Some of you will already have dismissed that as a significant understatement! But for those who are still with me here, what might some of the consequences be, supposing that I am even half right?

One conclusion would certainly be that we should be more generous about church styles that are not our own preferred forms. In spite of much progress through formal ecumenical collaborations, as well as with more informal alliances at local level, this is likely to prove quite challenging, if only because our various denominational traditions really have no reason to exist apart from an unspoken conviction that each one has a better version of the Gospel than the others, or has access to some different form of grace than anyone else. I wonder if we also lose something of value when we try to homogenize the Church into just one model. The formal ecumenical movement gave up on that long ago, but the attempt to create a hybrid lives on at congregational level all over the Global North, as traditional churches try to make themselves more trendy by incorporating contemporary worship songs originating from the charismatic section of the Church, and some charismatic churches for their part attempt to reintroduce forms of ancient rituals and liturgies. True integration almost never happens, hence the many references to 'worship wars', which is a shorthand way of saying that nobody feels truly at home. Those whose spirituality is nurtured through the inherited tradition find themselves distracted by the introduction of styles that mean nothing to them, while those who are nurtured by praise and worship music claim they are held back by what they regard as arcane and meaningless tradition. When that happens, both groups find themselves disempowered and consequently reluctant to even think that others like them who are not yet Christian might wish to connect with the Church. The concern to be 'relevant' is destroying many churches, when the call of the Gospel is to be 'incarnational', which among other things means we will take seriously the different ways in which those we may wish to reach are already seeking to connect with whatever it is that they regard as 'spiritual'.

There is also a major challenge here for the ways in which we articulate what the Gospel actually is. For generations now, the

Western world (and therefore Christian theology) has been obsessed
with life after death, and that still tends to feature in most, if not all,
presentations of the Gospel. It was noted in a previous chapter that
we live increasingly in an atmosphere of fearfulness, but that is more
likely to focus around the survival of the planet, or the human
species, rather than on personal survival beyond death. It is no
coincidence that so much attention in the wider culture is now
focused on a spirituality of life and lifestyle. The truth is that today's
people are more afraid of living than they are of dying. For proof of
that, we need look no further than the rising suicide rates among
people of all ages, but especially the young. In the opening sequence
of the movie *Suicide Club*, 54 high-school students line up on the
platform of a train station and jump simultaneously as the train
approaches – not as an act of desperation, but as a lifestyle choice. A
trend that started in Japan is now spreading throughout the world,
as individuals make suicide pacts in online chat rooms and then
meet up in order to carry it through.[23] In a project based at the
University of Edinburgh, Fergus Macdonald (a former General
Secretary of the United Bible Societies) has been researching Scripture engagement among young adults on and beyond the fringe of
the churches. As part of this, he recruited a broad cross-section of
students who committed themselves to reading the Psalms over a
period of time, using a form of *lectio divina*. In the process, six key
characteristics emerged that dominated their aspirations in life: to
have a good time (hedonistic); to be well thought of (to be liked and
have friends); to resolve pain (a wish to avoid suffering); to value
personal experience very highly as a source of truth-seeking; a
suspicion of institutions (scepticism); and an interest in engaging
with the ambiguity of life (questioning).[24]

There is a major challenge here for mission in a generation for
whom spiritual meaning starts with lifestyle issues. We have some
idea how to journey with people on matters of belief or mystical
experience, but how will we accompany those whose priority is first
and foremost a lifestyle question? We have a long history of walking
alongside people who come to us through the route of believing, and
have worked hard at starting with belonging. But can we make the
same accommodation for those whose primary concern is with living? Attentive readers will realize that this is where I make the
connection with my wife's work on *Spirituality to Go*. Actually, this is
a reinvention of some very ancient church practices, that can be
traced back in codified form at least to the third-century text

associated with the name of Hippolytus (the *Apostolic Tradition*), and further back still to the second-century *Didache* and the *Epistle to Diognetus*, and ultimately to Jesus' way of forming disciples.[25] I am not suggesting that we recycle these ancient catechetical tools for today's people, because their specific exhortations belong to their own age, but there is a pattern that we have something to learn from in these early examples. As Richard Rohr succinctly expresses it:

> Christians do not think their way into a new life; they live their way into a new kind of thinking.[26]

If I am correct in identifying this lifestyle (or ethical) route as a major transition point into Christian faith, then we may also need to revisit some classic understandings of the nature of faith itself, and how it develops and is nurtured. Writers like James Fowler and John H. Westerhoff have made significant contributions to our understanding of the relationship between personal development and the growth of faith. Their insights have not always been well received, and Fowler in particular has been criticized for operating on the basis of an exclusively male way of doing things (something that he has acknowledged, and taken steps to address). But it is also notable that all their models originated in an age when the influence of Christendom was still strong in Western societies.[27] In that context there was an assumption that 'belief about' would generally precede 'belief in', and individual faith could therefore be described in terms of moving from an inherited faith (inherited from the culture, or one's family) to an owned faith (internalized into one's own worldview and lifestyle). Insofar as these developmental theories used traditional terms like 'conversion', the sort of radical change encapsulated by such notions would have been identified with the transition into owned faith as something that permeated and informed the whole of life. But today this is no longer the case for those (the majority) who have never had any exposure to Christian belief in their upbringing, and I wonder if we are not now back in a situation more like the first century, when experience (of Christ and of the community of faith) was the first step and it was only on the basis of this that anyone bothered to explore the factual basis of discipleship. Might it be that some people today are being 'converted' first (by adopting a faith-integrated lifestyle) and then exploring the content of inherited faith not as the starting point of their spiritual journey, but as a subsequent stage as they reflect on how and why their life has taken a new direction? If this is indeed the case, then the entry point into Christian faith for people like that will not begin with doctrine or traditional apologetics (or the Alpha course) but with practices such as prayer, meditation, healing, and other things that begin with the agenda of those who are asking the questions of purpose and identity, rather than with the agenda of the Church.

I hope it is clear that I am not suggesting that we can expect or should encourage single-track discipleship, with Christians who behave, but do not believe, or who belong but do not behave, or whatever other combinations may be possible. Rather, I am saying that it is the lack of integration of these things that lies at the heart of much of the *angst* being experienced by so many people today, and if the Gospel cannot redeem that, then why would we expect anyone to bother, given all the existing pressures of our 24/7 lives? Here is another diagram to illustrate what I am thinking:

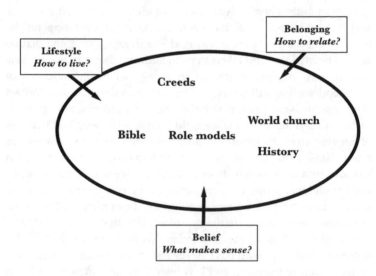

It envisages the entirety of the Christian tradition as being like a room, with different doors through which people might choose to enter. Some will come in because of their fascination with belief systems, and their starting point will be cerebral and cognitive, maybe even intellectual. C. S. Lewis was one such convert: he was intellectually convinced, but emotionally unsure, and described himself at the time as being 'the most dejected and reluctant convert in all England'.[28] Others will encounter the Christian tradition through their desire for community, while yet others will be looking to reinvent their lifestyle in empowering and nurturing ways. But once inside, all will discover other connections and possibilities that represent the richness of a historical tradition that will both expand and challenge expectations in a way that itself can be holistic and life-giving.[29]

I hardly need to point out that this will also require a change of gear, if not of direction, on the part of many Christians. For generations, we have understood mission in terms of revivalism, as if it is a matter of inviting those who are not yet Christian to return to their spiritual home, and they will do so if only we work hard enough, or manage to invent (or buy) the right programme to speak to their needs. But this approach assumes that the culture of Christendom still exists, and that there is still an underlying current of Christian belief influencing the general population of the Global North. To believe that is a form of denial, for the vast majority of people have no idea at all of Christianity, whether that be defined in terms of beliefs, practices, or lifestyle issues. You cannot call people back to something they have never had. Stuart Murray's advice that we ought to 'Stop praying for revival' might sound extreme, but he is right when he points out that this mind-set creates 'unrealistic expectations that foster disillusionment and hinder contextual missionary engagement'.[30] Of course, journeying with people in the way that is commended here is bound to be threatening, not least because it is impossible to walk alongside another person without revealing one's own vulnerabilities. It also requires us to be more self-consciously dependent on God, which is why the concept of the *missio Dei* is so central to everything here.[31] Lesslie Newbigin once observed that the Church has tended 'to make mission a burden rather than a joy, to make it part of the law rather than part of the gospel'.[32] A major reason for that is that mission has been regarded as an essentially human activity, for which we need to enlist divine help through intense prayer, whereas a more faithfully biblical understanding would see mission as a divine activity that invites human collaboration. There is a world of difference between the two, not only conceptually but also in practical terms. For if mission is something that we do, then we can stay firmly in control of it and, to some extent, predetermine its outcomes so they never challenge us beyond our own comfort zones. But if God is the initiator of mission, who knows where that might lead us, and what the outcome might be? A greater recognition of the many diverse ways in which God works in people's lives, and a willingness to embrace what God is doing, offers a way of doing mission that will certainly be scary but probably transformational, for Christians as well as for others. It is of course a return to a very old paradigm because it is grounded in the example of Jesus himself. What that might mean in relation to the ongoing ministry of the Church is the subject of our next chapter.

4 MINISTRY

Christian ministry today, at least in the countries of the Global North, must be one of the toughest jobs on the planet, especially for those who are involved in leadership at the level of the local congregation. It is in the local scene that the cultural challenges highlighted in previous chapters really make a difference to church life and vitality. It is undeniable that some local churches are thriving, and it would not be too difficult to fill this chapter with stories of congregations that have grown, in both quality and quantity. The flip-side of that equation is that one church's growth is often a direct consequence of another congregation's decline, as Christians regard faith as a consumerist choice, and opt for the sort of church that will best meet their perceived needs for a spiritual home. It is this phenomenon that to a large extent explains the rise of the megachurch. In its original definition (a church of more than 2000 members), this is still a predominantly American phenomenon, but if we make adjustments in relation to the population base and overall levels of churchgoing, the growth of churches that were already large to become bigger still can be tracked in other parts of the Global North as well. The trend is clearly exemplified in England, where 25 per cent of all churchgoers worship in only 4 per cent of churches, all of which have congregations of more than 400 (small by world standards, but large for England, where 75 per cent of churches have attendances of 100 or less), though the very largest of them have congregations in five figures.[1]

Church, ministry, society

It is easy to criticize those who shop for a church, and who choose to connect with one that is rich and successful rather than with a smaller church that may be facing greater struggles. But there are many reasons why people make such choices. My own experience suggests that larger churches are, on the whole, more intentional about welcoming strangers, and small churches often stay that way because they are intrinsically inhospitable, and not infrequently dominated by introspective cliques of people with no interest in other Christians, let alone those who may be outside the Church. For many people, though, a major attraction of a large church is that it tends to offer opportunities for the nurture of children, who can be part of a sizeable group of Christian peers within which their faith can be encouraged in ways that would be unlikely to happen in a church with few children or young people. Others find that the stresses and strains of a 24/7 lifestyle, and the phenomenon of being rich in cash but poor in time, means that many people are simply unable to offer the sort of investment in voluntary service that a small congregation might demand, though they are happy to give financial support to large ministry teams that can, in effect, do on a full-time basis what might in a different social setting be the work of volunteers. Single people likewise typically find that a large church can offer the chance to meet others who are single, without feeling pressurized to conform to stereotypes based on a norm of married life.[2] When we look at the bigger picture, of course, it soon becomes clear that we are taking false comfort from the growth of larger churches, for the underlying reality is that the number of Christians in the population has been in decline in the whole of the Global North for about the last 40 years, and what can be made to look like church growth actually amounts to nothing more than a movement of people who for the most part are already Christian.

Actually, the vast majority of churches are not particularly big. In both Britain and America, the average church has fewer than 100 regular attenders or members, though the precise figures vary depending on denomination (Roman Catholic churches tend to be bigger than Protestant ones) and the way in which the statistics are gathered (increasingly, figures relating only to attendance on a Sunday are not reflective of a church's true numerical strength or its impact in the community). It is the challenges facing leaders in these average churches that I want to focus on in this chapter. What I have to say does certainly contain some lessons for the leaders of larger churches, but they are not my main concern here.

In the course of the last four or five years, I have been involved in countless seminars for clergy of many different denominations and in many different countries. Though everyone seems to think that their problems are unique to their local situation, or even to their denomination or theological perspective, the one thing that has struck me over and over again is how we are all wrestling with what, in the end, are variations on a theme. The terminology might be different, and the theological understandings of what ministry is can be various, but at the point where it impinges on our daily life, the same concerns are voiced just about everywhere. There is no shortage of disillusioned people in ministry, who feel that they are misunderstood and undervalued by either their denominational superiors or their parishioners, and quite often by both. No wonder so many ministers are hanging on by their fingertips, aware of the need for change yet desperately hoping they can hold things together as they are until they themselves reach retirement age, and after that it will be someone else's problem. Those who are not within sight of their pension see a move to another church as a possible solution, or simply leave full-time ministry for another position, either in chaplaincy work or outside the Church altogether. Behind this there is often a sense of both disempowerment and bereavement – bereavement because the church in which we were trained to minister no longer seems to exist, and disempowerment because the skills that were once deemed to be central to a good theological education, and which have been carefully honed in a lifetime of faithful service, now seem to be at best irrelevant, and at worst might even be viewed as a contributory factor in church decline. Not long ago, I had a conversation with a retired church executive, who had been responsible for the pastoral care of ministers in his particular denomination, and who therefore had plenty of firsthand experience of the sort of frustration I have described here. His explanation was that those who are in ministry today have been trained to be 'pastors and teachers', following the sort of New Testament pattern hinted at in Ephesians 4:11, and for that reason have no idea how to operate in the sort of missional context that we now face. Someone else might have put it differently: that ministers have been trained to operate in the world of Christendom, where people automatically regarded themselves as Christians and the clergy were there to service their spiritual needs, and mission – if it ever happened – was based on a revivalist model that called people back to the faithful observance of a faith from which they had lapsed. Either way, such church leaders knew how to operate in a settled world in which people came to the Church seeking care, support, and spiritual direction. But now that we are in a different situation, and people will not generally come to the Church as a matter of course, such individuals are left high and dry, not quite knowing what to do, except what they have always done, which for large numbers means they end up running the spiritual equivalent of a hospice, caring for older people in the twilight of their lives, and being correspondingly overburdened with more than their share of funeral services, not to mention the depression that easily sets in with the realization that we are only reaching a tiny proportion of the population, most of whom will soon be dead. The executive I have just mentioned took the easy way out: although he recognized a need to address this situation, he chose to do nothing about it in relation to the training of ministers in his own denominational college, and supported the *status quo* until his retirement, after which it became his successor's problem (who, faced with a near-impossible task, will only manage to survive by repeating the same cycle of denial himself). When confronted by this sort of challenge, the thing that surprises me is not that a large number of clergy are angry and disillusioned, but that so many are still sane. Though denominational leaders mostly recognize the reality of these tensions, the ways in which the issues tend to be raised are not necessarily helping matters. CPD, CME and a host of other acronyms have become the buzz-words of contemporary ministry, as they have in every other area of professional life. But unlike commercial organizations, the Church typically allocates an insufficient amount of time to addressing such matters in ways that can really make a difference. For someone whose entire professional expertise is now being called into question, a one-day seminar even two or three times a year is not going to begin to address the matter, especially if such seminars have different guest facilitators on each occasion. It generally takes at least a day just to create the sort of safe space that is necessary for people to begin to open up and even acknowledge the existence and strength of their fears, with the result that all too often the only thing that happens at these events is a fresh articulation of the problem without any space for practical resolutions to be explored. The same can be said of the sort of sabbatical arrangements that many ministers are offered. When you are quite as burned out as some now are, it can take a couple of months of just being away from the job before it really feels as if you are actually on sabbatical, and so if the sabbatical itself lasts for only two or three months, it is going to come to an end at the very point where it might be most beneficial in terms of the sort of personal reassessment of priorities that could help hard-pressed church leaders see new possibilities for themselves and their congregations.

Local churches and their leaders

The struggles of the clergy cannot be understood in isolation, but need to be viewed alongside the pressures faced by everyone else. No one is immune from the sort of cultural anxiety identified in previous chapters. We all live within a rapidly changing context, and for many the Church has become a haven of relative calm in the midst of an otherwise out-of-control existential storm. It is easy to criticize those lay members of church councils and committees who resist any sort of reappraisal of the church's life, and to depict them as awkward or uncommitted people who want to hold back the work of God. But things are not so simple here either. In most churches today, the lay leaders are largely middle-aged to older people – even, in my experience, in churches that have significant numbers of younger people. In recent years, my wife has done some work as a mission consultant to a group of 14 churches in north-east Scotland and the Shetland Islands. She paid a visit unannounced to a young adults' group in one of these churches, just to get a feel for what was going on. Somewhat to her surprise, she found a significant number of people in their twenties, one of whom was the leader of this group, a position that he expected to have to relinquish once he reached the age of 30. His question to her was: what can I do with my life between then and when I am 50? I doubt that anyone had actually spelled it out as a policy, but that young man's observation was that only people of that sort of age and older got to be a part of the central leadership body of his particular church. That was the natural default position in that congregation, as a result of which he felt he would be in a sort of spiritual limbo until he reached middle age. But if he follows the prevailing trend, he will not still be in the church by the time he is 50. Other churches have virtually no younger people in them, and they tell me that if only they did, they would be appointed to leadership positions without any hesitation. The problem for many of these churches is that in the past, when they did have young people, they thought differently, and it was only the middle-aged and older members who were taken seriously. Even as I have been writing this chapter, one of my wife's students at Fuller Seminary, who is employed as a youth minister, shared with us something of the leadership discussion that was taking place in his own church. The senior minister of this church had been in post for more than 30 years, and by all accounts had done a good job. But now he was retiring, and the church (a parish of a mainline denomination) needed to decide on its next move. All the evidence (and there is plenty of it) shows that the person who follows a ministry of that length is likely to be in post for only a very short space of time. This usually has no connection with the competence or skills of the new minister, but stems from the fact that such congregations need a time of mourning to deal with what they have lost before being in a position to move on to something new. Individuals who find themselves in this situation always live under the shadow of their predecessor, and are regularly judged because they are different. This is a major reason why some denominations now use interim ministers as a matter of course, to create a space in which congregations can mourn for what they have lost, and move on in new ways without a long-term commitment. In this particular church, though, the youth minister had proposed what seemed to me to be a most creative idea. He noted that the retiring senior minister had enjoyed a stipend of $150,000 per annum (UK readers, eat your heart out – this was southern California!), and suggested that, for the same money, the church could appoint three people who would still have a good income at $50,000 each, and who might also have different skills that would diversify the church's ministries in ways that would enhance its presence in the community. His argument was partly based on knowledge of the difficulty of one individual ever replacing a long-term pastor, but also on the reality that the needs of both the church and its community had undergone significant change in the last 30 years, and what had been an appropriate model of ministry for the 1970s was no longer the best option. There was only one other person who was even prepared to countenance the possibility that this might indeed be a good idea. The search committee that was working to discern a way forward could understand well enough the reasoning behind it, even agreeing that a long-term ministry was a hard act to follow. But the proposal never got off the ground. I couldn't help but reflect that this same young person, when he was in one of my classes a couple of years ago, had told me that the leaders of this same church had employed him as a youth minister, with an expectation that he would be in the church nine-to-five every day. How, he asked then, did they expect him to reach young people from an office?

Why do otherwise intelligent people make such silly judgements when they are in the church, especially when (as is generally the case) they do not appear to live the rest of their lives like this? The sort of mid-life person now in leadership is likely to have been active in the Church for much, if not all, of their adult life. They have depended on their predecessors on boards and committees, and previous generations of clergy, to guide them in their spiritual journey. They have been obedient to all that the Church advised them to do – and, in very many cases (maybe the majority) it has not worked out as they were led to expect that it would. Nowhere is this more frequently the case than in relation to the children of people now in their fifties and sixties, who for the most part left the Church in their teenage years, or even earlier, and show no signs of returning. This is such a common scenario that it is now more likely that children brought up in the Church will leave it than that they will stay. In many instances, the challenge is compounded by the fact that such young people still maintain a faith in Jesus, and quite possibly continue in disciplines of prayer, Bible reading, and more – but say it is the Church and its ways (often what they regard as its hypocrisy) that they find distasteful. At a recent series of weekend seminars that my wife and I led for a church in the suburbs of Glasgow, it was suggested to those present who had adult children in this situation that they ask them what it would take for them to return to the Church. The answers brought back the following day were very revealing, as well as being remarkably consistent and straightforward. Without exception, these church leavers said that the problem was not with the seating, or the music, or the sermons, or the liturgy, but with the acrimonious way in which church people related to one another. Those who are living with this sort of family story typically do one of two things: they either leave the Church themselves (and growing numbers of older people are doing precisely this), or they live in tacit denial of the reality, a course of action that often spills over into anger because in their heart of hearts they feel let down by the Church but have no forum in which to express – still less to resolve – their frustration. Similar scenarios are played out in relation to the breakdown of relationships, divorce, and any number of other human experiences that challenge what they have previously understood of the Church and its teachings. If ministers need safe spaces in which to confront their own fears, then so too do the majority of lay people in all our churches. As surely as night follows day, personal pain among the people of God will inevitably lead to expressions of public anger that create dysfunction in the church community, and undermine even the best missional intentions.

An expanding part of my own ministry has been working with local churches to help them think through the sort of issues raised in

my writings on church and culture, and one of the most discoura-
ging aspects of that is to see just how much anger there is pent up in
so many churches, for these and similar reasons. Anger *per se* is not
necessarily a bad thing, and as I hear the stories of both clergy and
lay people, I have to conclude that many have good reason to feel
angry at the way in which they have experienced church life. But we
need to face up to our anger, learn to be honest about how we feel,
and deal with it. Avoidance is not a sensible option, and living in
denial will only make matters worse. Moreover, this is not just an
internal church matter, but has serious missional repercussions in
the form of this question that I regularly encourage leaders to consider: why would anyone wish to become part of a church full of
angry people? The church mentioned in the previous paragraph
gave me a striking example of this even while I was in the process of
writing this chapter. The workshop described there was on a
Saturday, and my wife was a guest preacher at the Sunday morning
service. The congregation consisted mostly of over-sixties, with a
smattering of people in their forties and fifties, and only one younger
couple who were probably in their mid-twenties. At the end of the
service, this couple paused to engage her in conversation about what
had been said in the sermon, and while she was talking with them at
the door of the church, I became aware of a commotion as older
people started to (literally) throw their weight around, muttering to
themselves that it was their church, and growling about these
incomers who were speaking with the minister and taking too long
to get outside and go home! Eventually one such older couple
physically barged their way through, stopped the conversation
dead, and effectively chased the younger ones from the premises. It
is hard to imagine that this couple would be back in a hurry, and all
my intuitions told me that those who were treated so disrespectfully
on that occasion would probably match the profiles of those who
formed the basis for Alan Jamieson's research on church leavers,
which demonstrated that it is frequently those who are most committed, and who could therefore make the greatest contribution to
enriching the life of the Church, who find themselves the most
marginalized.[3] Yet those same older people had sat in a seminar the
day before and bemoaned the fact that they never saw new faces in
their church! I wonder why? Ministry and mission are two sides of
the same coin, which is why much of what was said in the previous
chapter on mission actually relates to the ministry of the local
church, and why in this chapter there is still an underlying concern

about mission. Mission can never be far from our thinking on ministry, if only for the commonsense reason that unless we learn to engage in effective mission, there will continue to be fewer and fewer people in our churches, with a consequent diminishing of both the need and opportunity for ministry in that context.

The business of change

At the heart of all this is the question of change. The often-heard insistence that 'nothing will change in my church' is one of the worst forms of self-deluding denial. The facts speak for themselves: in the last 40 years, all our churches have changed, and continue to do so, mostly for the worse. Change is now endemic in the culture, for all the reasons spelled out in the first two chapters of this book. In the past, change tended to happen in a gradual and orderly fashion, as one generation succeeded another and built upon the wisdom of those who had gone before. Today, change is dramatic, sudden, and unpredictable, and the wisdom of the past does not always serve us well as we try to adapt to new conditions. The very foundations of Western culture are being shaken as never before, and even the institutions of government are creaking as we find ourselves ever more distrustful not just of politicians but of the systems within which they operate. The Church is no different, and the changes now sweeping through the Christian world are as unpredictable and threatening as any challenge that might be facing the wider culture. Old certainties are disappearing, and hallowed ways of doing things no longer resonate with those who are now in the Church, let alone those who are as yet not Christian. The question is not whether the Church will change, but whether we will be intentional about being part of the change, so that what happens is not imposed on us by external forces, but truly reflects the values of the Gospel. We live in a scary time, a time in which we are being called to reimagine much that once was thought to be settled and fixed, a time of great opportunity as well as of enormous challenge.

Saying all that is the easy part! How might ministry evolve in such a way as to engender and encourage the sort of change that will be faithful to the message of Jesus and contextualized within the culture? There are two ways of looking at leadership in the Church. One is by examining the practicalities of what church leaders do on a daily basis, and the other is by asking a more fundamental set of questions about the nature of the Church and through that identifying not only what tasks might need to be done, but the ethos and attitudes that should characterize our ministry. In what follows, I propose to include both these questions, because as I hear hard-pressed leaders complaining about how their time is taken up, I often find myself thinking that the problem is not intrinsically about time management, people skills, or any of the other things that are named, but that they are being required or expected (or, frequently, requiring of themselves) to do things that are either inappropriate or, in some cases, inimical to the Gospel they serve. I therefore want to begin with some fundamental reflections on what we are sup-posed to be about, before offering some practical observations on how hard-pressed leaders (whether clergy or lay) can get through from one day to the next without becoming either oppressed or destroyed in the process.

In Chapter 1, I made mention of the book *The Experience Economy*, by B. Joseph Pine and James H. Gilmore.[4] I am not one of those people who believe that the simple application of business models to church life is going to be the answer to the challenges we now face. On the contrary, it seems to me that the adoption of management techniques has in many cases diverted church leaders from their main task and calling, and has reduced to managers of bureaucratic systems those who should be heralds of an altogether different style of being. Nevertheless, I would also wish to affirm that there is no distinction between the sacred and the secular, which means that we ought to be able to discern signs of God at work in many different places. If you can manage not to be put off by the fact that they use the language of the marketplace (they are, after all, business pro-fessors), Pine and Gilmore offer a helpful perspective for thinking through the purpose of the Church and its ministries.[5] The passage I quoted previously highlighted the importance of what they call 'the transformation business'. Choosing the example of a fitness centre, they ask what its purpose might be, in terms of the question, 'what are people being charged for?' Though a fitness club might advertise itself as offering physical and psychological transformation in the lives of its members, Pine and Gilmore question whether most of them are 'truly in the transformation business', on the grounds that if they were then they wouldn't be charging membership fees, because that only gives people access to the tools of transformation. Instead, a health club that was serious about its mission to transform people's lives would charge for meeting the health and well-being aspirations of its members. If the aspirations were not met within a fixed period of time, the fitness center would not be paid – or it would be paid less, on some sliding scale commensurate with the progress achieved. In other words, it would charge not for the pain but for the gain.[6]

They continue by offering a list of different ways of doing business, by reference to what customers are paying for:

You really are what you charge for ... If you charge for *stuff*, then you are in the *commodity* business. If you charge for *tangible things*, then you are in the *goods* business. If you charge for *the activities you execute*, then you are in the *service* business. If you charge for *the time customers spend with you*, then you are in the *experience* business. If you charge for *the demonstrated outcome the customer achieves*, then and only then are you in the *transformation* business.[7]

This is not the way we have been taught to think of the Church, but I invite you to suspend your suspicions for a moment and reflect on it anyway. Using this taxonomy, what is the 'product' that the Church is offering to the public? My hunches incline me to think that most of the churches I come across see themselves as operating somewhere between what are called here the service business and the experience business, with most energy going into the former ('the activities you execute'). We need to ask ourselves: is this what the Gospel is supposed to be about? Or should we not rather be engaged wholeheartedly, and without diversion, in what Pine and Gilmore call the transformation business? The advice they offer to people who wish to facilitate transformation in the lives of others is a very risky strategy: because they would be paid only on the basis of the outcome, it involves an act of faith in having sufficient confidence in their product that they will, in effect, offer it for nothing at the point of delivery. This has interesting and close parallels with a central theological theme of the Christian faith, for on this definition transformational businesses could be understood as covenantal, an act of grace freely given and to which those whose lives have been transformed will respond with an offering of thanksgiving and commitment.

Is that pushing the analogy too far? Maybe – and in any case, all metaphors break down eventually, and I can already hear some readers reminding me that the transformations wrought by the

Gospel depend not on us, but on God. I agree with that. But the question with which I began this section is still a very good one: what is the 'product' that the Church is offering, to those presently outside the Church as well as to its own members? Have we lost sight of some fundamental reasons why the Church exists at all, and is it because we have lost confidence in the transformational power of the Gospel that we tend to focus on other things? And is that related to the repeated claim from spiritual searchers, that they want to be 'spiritual' but not 'religious' (because they do not see the Church as being in the transformation business, whereas other spiritual pathways evidently are, or seem to be)?

Leadership, power, control

Part of the difficulty that we face stems from the models of leadership that the Church has inherited, and usually embraced. Many clergy – and not a few laity – seem to share a deeply ingrained belief in the 'heroic leader', the sort of person who seems to be able to change the world single-handedly, and who appears to be totally self-motivated, with endless reserves of energy and inspiration even (or especially) when the going gets tough. This style of leadership occupies an almost archetypal position within the human psyche, and is the sort of leader who regularly appears in the traditional myths and legends of many cultures. Contemporary celebrity icons are often understood in this way, whether they be moral giants like Martin Luther King Jr and Mother Teresa of Calcutta, or the captains of sports teams, pop idols, or even fictional characters such as Gandalf, Harry Potter, or Spiderman. Alongside this – and partly in reaction against it – there has been a great deal of emphasis in recent years on so-called 'servant leadership'. Without necessarily naming it as such, many churches seem to operate on a very narrow spectrum of leadership styles that accommodates only these two extremes of servant or hero, with one or the other winning out at different times and places. No wonder then that many ministers find themselves uncertain about who they are meant to be, and what they might aspire to. It seems to me, though, that this is entirely the wrong way in which we should be thinking of leadership in relation to ministry. Neither of these styles is either workable or – more importantly – biblical.

The notion of a 'servant leader' has become trendy in the business world, something that automatically raises concerns for some

Christians,[8] though others argue that the best examples of business leadership are a form of implicit, or unrecognized, Christianity.[9] Much of what is presented in the literature as 'servant leadership' does indeed reflect some insights that are also to be found in the New Testament, though there is rarely any explicit connection made between the two. The theory proposes the rejection of a hierarchical form of leadership, in which decision-making happens at the highest level and is then handed down to lower levels, and substituting a linear model in which no one is either higher or lower in status than anyone else. In practice, of course, this egalitarian scheme never works quite like that, any more than St Paul's insistence that all parts of the body are of equal value means that all functions are of equal importance (1 Cor. 12:1–31). The key thing seems to be a rejection of a domineering form of leadership, with leaders taking specific steps to let go of the desire to control, while still remaining accountable and focused on the central tasks of leadership. This image is often promoted by the use of slick catchphrases, such as 'A servant leader is one who both serves by leading and leads by serving' – and it is possible to argue that Jesus provided the quintessential model for this, when he washed the feet of his disciples (John 13:1–20). But this notion is a construct that has been artificially created out of faulty exegesis of certain New Testament passages that, when correctly understood, are either not about leadership at all, or else are based on a different understanding of what it means to be the Church than the one we currently work with. Moreover, the use of this terminology conjures up images that are unhelpful in the context of Christian ministry in today's world, and easily reinforces the notion that effective leadership consists of service to the congregation, and maybe peripherally to the wider community. It tends to regard ministry primarily as pastoral support and care-giving, and those who adopt this model frequently find themselves spending much of their time visiting people, and generally being at the beck and call of anyone who thinks they have a problem. This expectation has no deep roots within the Christian tradition, and in historical perspective can be seen to be a relatively recent phenomenon, owing more to modernity's emphasis on the individual self as the centre of all things than to any biblical or theological understandings. Conversely, the notion of the heroic leader, who is omnicompetent both to address and to deal with any issue that might arise, is to a large extent a legacy of Christendom, when power over others (or on behalf of others) came to be a key defining characteristic of the

Church – though more recently it has been combined with ideas from the corporate world that regard the minister as the CEO of his or her local parish or congregation. Here again, it is hard to find any biblical or theological justification for this way of being.

Quite apart from whatever theoretical notions might lie behind these images of leadership, we should also take note of the simple fact that neither model actually works very well in practice. 'Servant leadership' often leads to a situation in which there is no effective leadership at all, and a church just goes round in circles like a rudderless ship, expending a lot of energy but going nowhere. Historic Presbyterianism offers a glimpse of this model in operation, with its tendency to hand decision-making on from one committee to another, with no one individual ever able to take responsibility for moving forward. It is no surprise that one of the largest Presbyterian denominations in the world (the Presbyterian Church of the USA) has established the position of regional 'executive presbyters' (bishops by any other name, perhaps?) as a way of breaking through that sort of deadlock. 'Heroic leadership', of course, all too easily descends into a form of bossiness, in which those who disagree with the leader can find themselves marginalized and abused. It can also soak up people's energy, with little to show for it, for it encourages a mindset that sets up committees, task-forces and projects as a way of demonstrating that the Church is doing 'real' work just like the business community. At a time when many people feel oppressed by such over-rationalized and McDonaldized systems in other areas of their life, this has missional implications, for who would wish to join an organization that offers just more of the same – not to mention the fact that the fundamental calling of the Church is not about activism, but is supposed to be focused on God?

Both these concepts are underwritten by a questionable under-standing of the nature of power, as if power was in short supply and there is only a limited amount of it to go round. We can be forgiven for supposing that this notion is rooted in some ontological reality in the structure of the cosmos, for all our inherited civic and social institutions operate on this assumption. But the idea that power – and therefore leadership – is accessible only to a select few enshrines a doctrine that is the exact opposite of the Gospel. For in biblical terminology, the good news is that we are all people made in the image of God, and that in our following of Jesus we can be empowered to fulfil that potential as our lives are transformed through the working of the Spirit. Leadership in this frame of reference then becomes a shared passion, in which we exercise 'power with' rather than 'power over' others. There is enough power to go round without it all needing to be in the hands of just a few individuals! Some denominational traditions like to think this is what they are already doing, notably those that have historically been grouped together as the 'free' or 'nonconformist' churches, though the practice rarely matches the theory as notions like 'the priesthood of all believers' can easily become an excuse for doing nothing, creating systems in which the buck is endlessly passed from one committee to another because nobody has been empowered to make ultimate decisions about anything – something that then tempts ministers to behave in autocratic and domineering ways, simply out of frustration and an understandable desire to see some progress.

The other side of this coin is that congregations can also be inclined to buy into this idea that power is a limited commodity, and therefore leadership is something that can be exercised only by a few special individuals, with most people being not leaders but followers. The structures of Christendom encouraged this sort of thinking, and the results are all too obvious in many churches, where congregations develop an unhealthy dependency on their clergy, and choose as lay leaders those individuals who will dispel their anxieties rather than the creative ones who will inspire and empower them to move in new directions. Whenever leadership is based on dependency, then the whole group is impoverished, whether it is a small local congregation or a large multinational organization. A biblical model of leadership – and therefore of ministry – involves everyone, and makes for a community that can shape its own future under God, while expecting itself to be restructured and changed in the process.

When we begin to think of ministry in this way, it takes us straight back to the question I raised earlier in this chapter, about the nature of the 'product' which the Church is offering. If the people of God are to play their part fully in ministry, then they must have a clear sense of what the Church is for, where it is going, and what their role within it might be. Once there is this sort of shared vision, it is not difficult for people to identify their own purpose and value within the Church, and to start to engage wholeheartedly in the life of faith. I have been around long enough to know that, however attractive it may sound in theory, this sort of leadership model is very scary for most full-time ministers. Though some fear a loss of personal power and a diminishing of their control over the congregation, the reasons for this are mostly connected with my starting point in this chapter – that is, the lack of openness in discussing these matters, and the near-total absence of any sort of effective training that will equip people to operate in this way within the Church. Even those who might look as if they are unredeemable control freaks can end up being like that just because they know of no other way to work within a congregational context, and are afraid of moving into unknown territory. It is, however, a misunderstanding to suppose that full-time leaders are no longer required. Given today's 24/7 lifestyles, and the consequential negative impact on volunteering, we might easily require more, not fewer, people in some form of paid ministry. We need individuals who can see the big picture, and have an overview not only of the interior life of the Church but also of the culture in which we operate, with a view to extending the ministry of the Church into areas that would otherwise be untouched. But if leadership is limited to only one person who does this, then not only is the view bound to be partial – even distorted – but that one individual is also likely to find his or her time fully occupied with only one aspect of the Church's life (usually the internal one) in a way that leaves no time for reflection on the missional challenges and opportunities, which is the one aspect of ministry that is absolutely crucial for the future of Christian witness in the countries of the Global North.

Moving forward

How then can we start to move from where we are to where we might need to be? The first step is always going to be the creation of a safe space where our true anxieties can be shared, accepted, and addressed in reflective and life-giving ways. People need to be given permission to name their fears without imposing on them the additional prospect that they might also be judged for being fearful. This invariably means that the process will have to start with those who are the recognized leaders of congregations, which usually means the clergy. In a structure that looks to ministers to resolve everything, the temptation is to come up with good ideas that seem as if they might address the challenges of falling attendance, ageing congregations, loss of young people, or whatever other issues we might be facing. The idea that the minister is some sort of expert in all these things can be both reinforced and created by even trivial things like the way we are described, or describe ourselves. It never ceases to both amaze and amuse me the way some churches announce on their noticeboards the degrees and other professional qualifications that their ministers hold – as if anyone in the wider world is the slightest bit interested in any of that. By encouraging the idea that those in full-time ministry are experts, and therefore everyone else is more or less ignorant and unqualified, we are creating a rod for our own backs, because (reasonably enough) we are then expected to come up with the answers. In today's consumerist culture, there is no shortage of individuals and organizations who know that the hard-pressed local clergyperson has little time for creative engagement with any of this, and offer ready-made solutions in the form of strategies and programmes that (of course) can be marketed and presented as the latest trendy thing that every growing church needs to engage with. I am old enough to have seen more than one or two such programmes come and go. At one time, it was church growth theories that were going to make a difference, based on the creation of homogeneous unit churches.[10] Then it was 'seeker-friendly' events, in which we were encouraged to create 'services' that would look as little like church as possible.[11] When it emerged that a fair number of people are actually interested in being spiritual, and are more interested in ancient liturgies and rituals than in quasi-religious theatre, 'alternative worship' was hailed as the latest big idea. The list could go on – and I haven't even mentioned the Alpha course and its various imitators. The point of saying this is not to denigrate these initiatives: no doubt they have all, in their own ways, been of some value, otherwise no one would ever have been interested in any of them for more than a second or two. But the fact that we feel a need to try one programme after another suggests that this approach is not as productive as those who sell these ideas would like us to believe – and it is certainly the case that the total number of Christians within the populations of the Western world has continued to decline, in spite of all the time and money that has been invested in such enterprises.

Some churches have bought into pre-packaged programmes more enthusiastically than others, but there can be very few that have not engaged in some development of their buildings in the effort to reconnect with a community that appears to have lost interest. I remember being at a major international conference at which a Christian leader exhorted us to do just that, using as his text a phrase purloined from the 1989 movie, *Field of Dreams*. In this film, Iowa farmer Ray Kinsella hears a voice in his corn-field telling him, 'If you build it, he will come.' He understands this to be an invitation to construct a baseball field, on which in due course appear the ghosts of Shoeless Joe Jackson and the other seven Chicago White Sox players who were banned from the game for conspiring to fix the outcome of the 1919 World Series. Unfortunately, such dreams only come true in the imagination of Hollywood movie directors. In the real world, churches that follow this sort of advice all too often end up investing a lot of money, time, and nervous energy, only to find themselves operating as a letting agent to community groups who use their premises but have no intrinsic connection with the spiritual life of the church.

There are two fundamental problems with this top-down approach to ministry: it is inappropriate in a post-modern cultural setting, and it pays insufficient attention to biblical styles of lea-dership. Incidentally, this has no bearing on theologies of ministry, and what I am saying here is as relevant to a high-church under-standing of priesthood as it is to a pastor in an independent evangelical congregation. What I am referring to here is not the ontological function of the clergy, but about style. The old Christendom-style paradigm, which placed ministers on a pedestal, has no future in the culture of the Global North. The underlying assumption on which it depends, with a clear demarcation between experts who know it all and other people who need it all, has long since been superseded. Of course, we value the insights of those who know about something that the rest of us are ignorant of, but the way we utilize such insights has changed forever. You only need to think of how we now regard physicians. At one time, they were among the most trusted groups in society, and patients consulted them not just to discover the nature of their illnesses but on a whole range of other relational matters. Nowadays, most people consult a website first, either to self-diagnose or, more often, to check out the appropriate treatment for their condition so they can know that when they consult the doctor they are being prescribed the right medications. It is not that we no longer use or value the expertise of those who have trained in medicine – we just use it in a different way, knowing that at the end of the day, a doctor is human like the rest of us. Most churches have a lot of running to do in order to catch up, as we simply do not know how to minister except from within a fixed framework, whether of dogma or practice, with which we expect others to conform. In the old world of modernity, it was possible to operate like this, because everything else in the culture worked that way. For the most part, this is still the paradigm within which churches operate. In the meantime, the daily lived reality of us all has changed beyond recognition. Moreover, it continues to change, not just in terms of the speed at which things happen, but even the nature of change itself is changing all the time. In this sort of environment, we need more than just cosmetic changes to our understandings of ministry. Albert Einstein is famously credited with having remarked that 'insanity is doing the same thing over and over again, and expecting different results'. His own achievements bear eloquent testimony to the fact that if you want different results, you have to think outside the box and operate on entirely different presuppositions. As it happens, this is precisely what the Gospel invites us to do. God's ways are not our ways, and the values of the Kingdom are supposed to undermine the world's ways so that the first become last, foolishness becomes wisdom, and those who are the least open up new vistas for those who think they are somebody. Could it possibly be that our top-down styles of ministry are actually part of the problem rather than part of its solution? Are we encouraging those who are in the Church to regard themselves as consumers of religious goodies purveyed by professionals, and in the process creating that disempowerment and dependency that leads to the isolation and over-work experienced by many ministers?

The road ahead

Where can we start to move forward? There are three indispensable elements around which Christian faith revolves: God, people, and the heritage of those who have gone before us (in Scripture and throughout history). I often describe these as three intersecting stories: God's story (the *missio Dei*), our stories, and Church stories. The first two are so interwoven with each other that we can think about them together. We need to begin with people, not least because people are the Church's most valuable tangible resource. More than that, people actually are the Church, and without people there could be no Church. What is the dominant story in people's lives today? Obviously, there is no single answer to that: people's stories are as diverse as the people themselves. But we can make some generalizations. Most people today find life much harder than their parents and grandparents did, with too much work and too little work both blighting the lives of large numbers of individuals. On top of that, there is a growing sense of uneasiness about the future, whether that is anxieties about terrorism, the future of the planet, or just where the next meal is coming from. For all the reasons identified in the first two chapters, people in the Global North have (in economic terms) never been better off, and yet never been so stressed. Christians are not exempt from all this, and the breakdown of relationships and other stress-inducing factors are as real for church members as they are for everyone else. In order to deal with this, we all need to be part of a story that is bigger than ourselves, and one of our difficulties is that the story that gave meaning to past generations no longer resonates with us. The claim of François Lyotard has achieved a sort of iconic status, with his characterization of post-modernity as 'incredulity toward meta-narratives'.[12] It is indeed the case that we have questioned, and largely rejected, the metanarrative of continual progress and the idea that science could or would solve all problems that inspired our forebears – because we now can see that, while that might once have corresponded to the reality of everyday life, that is no longer the case in relation to life as we experience it today. But things are more complex than that, because what has actually happened is that we have exchanged a metanarrative that was too simplistic and over-rationalized for one that tries to take account of life's complexities, but which ends up seeing little or no meaning or coherence in anything. It is no coincidence that there is widespread fascination with ancient esoteric mythology, with its origins in worldviews that are often magical and animistic (or certainly not inspired by Cartesian rationalism). Nor is this the preserve of the educated middle-classes who have nothing to do but think about such things: many computer games are also based on the same sort of ancient stories and mysteries. Faced with the collapse of the metanarrative of modernity, we do not automatically abandon the belief that there might be a big story that can give meaning to our own personal stories. When the overarching story of the culture is one of chaos and fragmentation, we either accept it and become chaotic and fragmented people, or we search for other stories that will offer hope and point the way to new definitions of wholeness.

This has to be a starting point for effective ministry. The story of Christendom is a part (though not the entirety) of the metanarrative that has been rejected, and that is a major reason why people say they have no time for the Church. But when they also say (as they frequently do) that they are attracted by Jesus, they are identifying something that Christians often miss. Taking Jesus as our model for ministry could be life-giving. In particular, we need to remember that Jesus always started where people were at, taking seriously their lived experience (their stories), and then inviting them to see things in the light of the bigger story of what God is doing. In our context, this will involve opening up a space in which people can see their own lives as the arena of God's activity, engaging in a continuous dialogue with Scripture, and reimagining the Church in the light of that experience. This may sound unexceptional and hardly innovative, but when we ask what might be involved it becomes far more radical than most of us appreciate. Notwithstanding statements to the contrary, many churches find it difficult to offer a space in which people can actually reflect on their personal stories in a way that enables them to see God at work. Alan Roxburgh and Fred Romanuk complain that people now go to church 'to listen to sermons, study the Bible, volunteer for programs, and pray for one another' but there is 'never a place where they could talk about the things churning inside them. All the questions about loss, history, and memory – their lived experience – didn't seem to have a place for expression', adding that 'until people can put their feelings into words and be heard, they are held captive by unarticulated anxiety'.[13] Just as we are in uncharted cultural territory today, so also we find ourselves in new spaces in relation to the discontinuities of our personal lives. If we are stressed, fragmented, and anxious, we will have to start with the brokenness of people, look to see where God is at work in that, and explore ways of connecting with the Bible narratives through the reality of our own experience. This is what Jesus did, as he met those who were struggling with life, and in the process of doing so he opened up new ways of seeing.

In the Italian city of Florence in 1501, a 26-year-old artist named Michelangelo Buonarroti eyed up a tall, narrow block of marble that had been abandoned by two other sculptors who regarded it as being so ruined that it had no possible value. Three years later, it had become a statue of the biblical king David that continues to be acclaimed as one of the greatest pieces of art ever created. Asked to explain himself, Michelangelo said that he always studied each block of stone until he understood the angel living inside it, and his job as an artist was to release that angel so as to enrich the lives of others. He did not, so far as I know, claim any specific divine inspiration for this process, but his language reflects the way in which Jesus worked with people. As a Christian, Michelangelo's chief aim was to glorify God, something he believed he was doing by depicting God's highest creation (people, made in God's image) as perfectly as was humanly possible. Jesus sees not only what a man or woman is, but also what he or she can become. He even used a building metaphor to imagine this (Matt. 7:24–27), though it is St Peter who complements Michelangelo's insight by reminding his readers that they are 'living stones' with a part to play in a structure that is bigger than any one of them (1 Pet. 2:4–5) – while other New Testament passages also utilize the same imagery (Eph. 2:19–22; Col. 2:6–7).[14]

This is the kind of mindset that will create the communities of transformation that we ought to aspire to. It can be developed not through trendy programmes but through a rediscovery of some basic elements of Christian spirituality and nurture. In our enthusiasm for trying to make the Gospel relevant to a changing culture, we have overlooked the fact that our calling is not to be relevant, but to be incarnational. Too often, the quest for relevance has ended up with the Church affirming the very aspects of the culture that are causing people so much anxiety in the first place. Instead of becoming disciple-making communities, we have encouraged a privatized view of faith that, of course, matches the culture – but misses the point of authentic following of Jesus. It is increasingly difficult to find a church whose worship is not at least partially contaminated by worship songs that are about me, my needs, and my own relationship with Christ (sometimes expressed in the sort of language that would be more appropriate between lovers than in public worship). The dumbing-down of worship has been well documented by other writers, but it is not just music that comes in for this treatment. I have noticed a trend in recent years for prayer to be relegated to a footnote in many church services (especially those of an evangelical persuasion), and much the same thing could be said about the place given to the Bible (and in the same sort of churches). A lot of preaching seems to be more like private therapy, as people are given bland nostrums to help them cope, rather than an invitation to serious encounter with the text, still less with God:

> Salvation in most Protestant sermons is a happening in the heart whereby individuals are restored to God's good grace by means of a personal decision for Jesus, have psychological peace, and hope of some heavenly hereafter.[15]

Richard Bewes (himself an evangelical) is more damning still, while making an important point about where God might most easily be found in the wider culture:

> Plenty of preaching in the West today is of an entertaining, joke-ridden nature; it is as if the church and the theatre have neatly swapped roles. It is the theatre that tends now to take on the big themes that speak to the dilemmas of humanity, while the biggest-selling tapes at Christian conferences will often be from the speakers with the best jokes and banter.[16]

All these trends can be traced to the Church's uncritical embracing of modernity with its focus on the individual self and its need for therapy through McDonaldized systems, which can of course look as if it is working for a while. But the longer-term outcome is now being realized, as many churches (especially, though not exclusively at the evangelical end of the spectrum) offer a diet that is spiritually damaging, serving up religious junk food that leaves people bloated and self-satisfied but still under-nourished in such a way that they never do find the angel trapped within, and have no opportunity to grow as fully integrated persons and disciples. This is a major reason why people leave churches, and why others are not attracted to them in the first place. It is something along these lines that people are trying to tell us when they say that the Church is not spiritual enough. In thinking about mission, I suggested that lifestyle issues are now becoming a major entry point for people to reflect on the meaning of life, and the possible relevance of Christian faith to their own existence. For some people, their reflections on the spirituality of lifestyle may be focused on matters of personal morality. Just recently, I found myself in conversation with a young woman at an emerging church in England. She told me that she had connected with this particular group of Christians when she started thinking about her relationships. Now in her late twenties, she had had more than 30 sexual partners since the age of 15, and she woke up one morning and just asked, 'What am I doing with my life?' She also wondered who might help her to change, and through networking with others in her place of employment she had connected with this church and had found them to be supportive of her desire for a new way of being. She told me quite frankly that she had no idea what, if anything, she believed in a theoretical sense about the Christian faith. But she had found acceptance and support, and for that reason was open to explore things more deeply. Actually, though she didn't name it as such, she was already well along the path to what in other terminology might be regarded as repentance and conversion. Others are asking different sorts of lifestyle questions, focused more on peace and justice, and the future of the planet. They too could conceivably make connections with Christians who are passionate about these things, none of which are in any way alien to the Gospel. Yet I still meet Christians who insist that none of this has anything to do with God. Not only are they missing an opportunity for significant ministry in a hurting world: they are also denying one of the fundamentals of biblical faith, for the very idea that there are no-go areas where God cannot be found is not merely sectarian, but is downright heretical. Even those who would not make that mistake, though, might still reflect on how we might facilitate those whose entry point into faith will come through lifestyle issues rather than belief systems or belonging to a group. I wonder if, in our understandable concern to attract as many people as possible, we might have made entry into the Church just a bit too easy. Presenting discipleship as something more demanding is not to be confused with the imposition of rules and regulations. That not only runs counter to the clear teaching of Jesus, but also ends up trivializing something that should be serious, and actually makes it quite undemanding, because keeping rules can be an easy thing for people who like to live that way. Discipleship, according to the New Testament, is altogether a more radical and far-reaching business. We have certainly done ourselves no favours by implying that being a Christian is something that can be done in an hour a week on Sundays, and for a generation that is now looking for a whole-life spirituality that can be a good enough reason for not taking church seriously at all, for how can anything of value make such insignificant demands? We are gradually coming to realize that much of what we thought we were doing to encourage seriousness in following Christ has not quite turned out the way we hoped. When Dan Brown's book *The Da Vinci Code* became so popular, two things surprised me.[17] One was that so many people in the wider public are still fascinated by the details of Christian history – and the other was that so few Christians seemed to have any idea at all as to how to engage with any of it. If sophisticated Christian education programmes have delivered so little wisdom, it must be time for a reappraisal of what we are doing. But then, it appears that the people who learn most from basic courses such as Alpha are not (as is widely assumed) interested non-Christians, but those who are already members of the Church.[18] I meet many ministers who tell me that they have faithfully taught their people through sermons week after week, and I have no reason to question the energy and commitment with which they do that. But if so few seem to have learned anything, even about fundamental matters such as the early history of the Church in New Testament times, then at the very least we are faced with a challenging question, if not a major problem. The notion of formal catechesis might sound dated to some, and anathema to others who think we have nothing to learn from the past, but it is at least a question worth thinking about.[19]

Leadership styles will be central in addressing the issues identified in this chapter. Jesus was, above all, a relational leader. He was neither the servant, being downtrodden by everyone else, nor was he the hero, telling others how it was supposed to be. He was neither below nor above, but alongside. As such, his presence and role were crucial, but his teaching was constantly interwoven with the insights of the disciples as they journeyed alongside one another. He knew that for spiritual growth to take place, the key question is not what we think we are teaching, but what we and others are learning – and for that to happen, we need to begin with our own and others' lived experience. We also need a revised model of what we believe theology to be, and that takes us on into our next and final chapter.

5 THEOLOGY

Theology can be an unpopular topic these days, among church people as well as in the wider culture. For much of the twentieth century, public perceptions of theology were generally negative, though mostly benign and good-humoured in character, regarding it as a curiosity belonging to a past generation and of diminishing relevance to a fast-changing world. Today, there is a widespread opinion that theology (usually identified with religious dogma) is a thoroughly bad thing, responsible for much of the worldwide strife that features in our news bulletins on a daily basis, and therefore to be critiqued at every possible opportunity – hence the rise of the sort of militant atheism that has not been seen since the eighteenth century, informed this time not by the speculations of philosophers, but backed up by what are claimed to be the hard facts of empirical science.[1] At one time, universities regarded theology as the 'queen of sciences' and its study served not only to prepare people for Christian ministry, but also to inform the value systems of our great national institutions. Much of that has now disappeared, and universities have not only relegated theology to the margins of intellectual inquiry, but have mostly revised their mission statements so as to be less value-driven and more market-oriented. As a direct consequence of that process, the teaching of Christian theology at every level of the educational system is being replaced by a relativistic pluralism, which reflects the many different value systems that can be found in the world, but is a process that makes it difficult, if not impossible, to have a sustainable and stable civic society. In the past, educators would have felt some responsibility for this, whereas nowadays most of them seem to be motivated by the desire (or need) to make money, and regard matters such as public values as being someone else's problem. It is one thing to create a society in which individuals will not be persecuted for their beliefs, but quite another to attempt to base a society on a model which accords equal status to everything, which of course means that nothing is the norm. The thinking behind this is regularly presented as a form of openness to other cultures, lifestyles, and beliefs than the traditional ones of the Global North, and therefore postures as a force for global liberation. The underlying reality, however, is quite the opposite and actually represents a marginalization of all belief systems in favour of a secular mindset that is engendering a form of ideological anarchy. For if (as is often taken for granted) all cultures are provisional and relative – and therefore nothing really means anything – then it is easy to appear to accept everything, because if everything is relative, then by definition everything is ultimately equally unimportant and meaningless (except the opinion that everything is relative, which is now the holy grail of Western academics and their political masters).

The marginalization of theology in the public square has its parallels within the churches, and over the last few years I have detected a distinct mood of suspicion towards anything that might be labelled theological and, by extension, towards those who would claim to be theologians. In a previous chapter, I made brief reference to my own experience of trying to integrate into churches in the north-east of Scotland, and there can be little doubt that a component in that was the fact that many churches at local level have a deep distrust of anything to do with theological enquiry. I have some limited sympathy with that viewpoint, because we have all come across self-opinionated 'experts' who think they know everything, and browbeat others into silence either through force of personality or merely by using complicated ways of speaking that are disconnected from ordinary life. But we do ourselves a disfavour by disallowing expertise, and the results of this are to be seen in the sort of church study groups that operate at a level of the lowest common denominator, and either never tackle the big questions being asked by those spiritual searchers whom the churches desperately need to reach, or become exercises in shared ignorance that satisfies no one. In addition to that, there is also the uncomfortable reality that such theological debate as there is in some churches (and not just at local level) tends to confirm the negative stereotypes of the subject that are held in the wider culture. I was recently involved in a consultation with a small group of world-class media people, and the question was raised as to whether the media presents a negative image of Christianity. One participant, who owns more than half the world's media outlets, denied this and pointed out that the media can only report what happens, which to him was a lot of wrangling between different interest groups about a host of matters that – to outsiders at least – look like trivialities, but which for those involved in them seem to have become life-and-death struggles (which is precisely why they are newsworthy). When politicians say (as they sometimes do) that they wish to avoid getting into 'theological' arguments about things, they are not usually referring to debates about God, but to this small-minded, hair-splitting way of discussion that somehow seems to have become identified with the very essence of theological conversations.

Words and meanings

In attempting to rehabilitate Christian theology, I am therefore under no illusion that in this chapter I am entering a minefield, and like many of those who have gone before, I will likely become the target of complaint and condemnation as a consequence. By way of setting the scene for what follows, it will be helpful to reflect briefly on the word itself. Like many Christian terms, the origin of the word 'theology' is to be found in ancient Greek, though the term itself never occurs anywhere in the Bible. It is formed of two Greek words, *theos* and *logos*, the one meaning 'God' (or 'god') and the other conventionally rendered into English as 'word' or 'idea'. The etymology of words *per se* is rarely a reliable guide to their meaning, and making that mistake is at the root of many of the more acrimonious arguments that are going on in church circles today, whether about the meaning of the atonement, or the ministry of women, or questions about sexual orientation. To understand what a word means, we need to look at how it is used. There are many examples of the difference between etymology and usage in contemporary English. For example, no one could reliably understand what people now mean by the words 'gay', 'cool', or 'wicked' merely by tracing their etymological roots.[2] To understand language, we need to look first at usage. There are very few occurrences of the term *theologos* even in ancient literature, but such as there are offer an interesting insight into the way it was originally understood. Philo of Alexandria, a Jewish philosopher who was a near contemporary of Jesus, describes Moses as a *theologos*, and the context makes it clear that the word highlights Moses' function as a spokesperson on behalf of God.[3] Other occurrences of the word in ancient inscriptions confirm something similar, namely that 'theology' (while, of course, being technically a noun) is to be regarded as something active, functionally almost a verb. It is a doing word, and in particular it is rooted in the idea that an individual communicates something of God to others. As I was reflecting on this, I naturally thought of the one context in the New Testament where the two constituent parts of the word *theologos* are indeed found in close proximity to one another. This is the prologue to the Fourth Gospel (with a parallel in the introductory paragraph of 1 John), where the *Logos* (Word) is identified with *Theos* (God), but then crucially both are identified with Jesus, in that central statement that 'the Word became flesh and lived among us' (John 1:14). Philo may have regarded Moses as God's herald, but Jesus is theology personified. God is not merely spoken of by Jesus, but is embodied in him. This seems to imply that anything claiming to be Christian theology must start – and end – with Jesus, not as an object of belief but as a personal manifestation of who God is. To regard Jesus in this personal way suggests that doing theology in its purest form will be a relational enterprise, and this is indeed precisely what we find in the way that Jesus taught, which from start to finish was relational rather than propositional. By turning theology into a largely intellectual hair-splitting exercise of the sort described previously, we disregard the incarnational nature of the Gospel and place ourselves in control of the whole process, thereby undermining the mutual relationality between ourselves and God in Christ that ought to be central to the whole enterprise. It then becomes possible to 'do theology' without any reference to persons and their needs, whether our own or those of others. It also, and tragically, becomes a simple matter to distance ourselves from the Jesus of the Gospels (who challenges us to behave like him), preferring instead a Jesus of the creeds (with whom we can agree or disagree at will). This surreptitious shift should be challenged, not just because of its rational ineptitude, but because it also lies at the heart of much of the Church's difficulties in mission today. This observation connects with what was said in Chapter 2 about the relationship between Christology (how we relate to Jesus), missiology (how we relate to the culture) and ecclesiology (what we think the Church is). It was suggested there that missiology ought always to be in the centre, but we will end up with very different understandings of it depending on which of the other two forms our starting point. The same can be said for theology: starting with Jesus and his vision of God's Kingdom offers a different orientation than starting with the Church and its internal concerns.

Before pursuing that, however, we need to unpack this a little more. Because of my involvement with the ecumenical movement, I have regular opportunities to minister in churches of many different denominational and theological traditions. But regardless of the context, two sorts of discussion crop up with predictable regularity. On the one hand, when I preach a sermon that includes exhortations to 'follow Jesus' – and especially if I suggest that Christians ought to model their own behaviour on his attitudes as recorded in the Gospels – there will invariably be someone who will remonstrate with me afterwards because they do not believe that the Gospels are to be regarded as a primary source of either belief or behaviour. Instead, they insist, the most important thing is what we believe *about Jesus*, and they most often regard St Paul as a better guide than the Gospel writers at this point. I do not happen to share their opinion about St Paul (whose style closely parallels that of Jesus), but I would still think that what we know of Jesus is likely to be of more central importance than what we think we understand of Paul.[4] On the other hand, I also meet Christians who find me frustrating precisely because I still want to take Scripture seriously, and so I end up being too radical for some and too conservative for others. Holding together thinking and doing, praxis and reflection does indeed introduce an ambivalence in what might be regarded as the essence of theology, but I for one am happy to live with that because I also wish to claim that it is impossible to do theology (as distinct from thinking about theologians) without also following Christ in faithful discipleship.

What I have just described explains why I regard myself as a 'practical theologian' rather than a theologian who happens to be practical. In adopting this terminology, I am well aware of the warning offered by Jeff Astley (another practical theologian), that

> any person or activity described as 'practical' runs the risk of being allowed into polite company only if they can show themselves to provide some useful service ... and then for no longer than it takes.[5]

I have been around long enough to know that the sort of polite company to which he refers (university common rooms and the likes) often exemplify Hans Christian Andersen's tale of the emperor's new clothes, with much pontification about things that nobody else cares about expressed in language that no one else can understand. At the same time, I can understand why scholars in the more traditional theological disciplines of biblical studies, systematic theology, and so on might have legitimate reasons to question practical theology's integrity as a discrete discipline. Not only is it to some extent a theological method that is still in the process of finding its identity, but it is certainly the case that in the past practical theology has not had much of a track record in terms of its capacity for paying serious attention to the Bible and the wider Christian tradition. Some of what passes for practical theology is not theology at all, but a mixture of second-hand notions gleaned from the edges of disciplines such as psychology, sociology, or healthcare, in which the Bible either never features at all or is treated in an unreflective way that verges on fundamentalism. I remember attending a seminar in 'practical theology' at which this question was asked: 'If Adam had fallen (i.e. tripped over) before the Fall, would he have skinned his knees?' The person leading it was a senior professor, and when he asked us what the answer might be, I thought he must have been joking, and said so. How wrong I was! My astonishment that anyone might even think of such a question was only overtaken by the fact that the group then spent a full two hours trying to answer this silly question, when even the average intelligent reader of the Bible would have recognized its naïvety in relation to the genre of the biblical literature. I immediately empathized with Lord (Professor) Robert Winston's opinion that 'The reason why the churches are so empty is that . . . they talk shallow nonsense to a highly literate society.'[6]

Practical theology

Though the term itself has only recently come into vogue to describe a particular way of doing theology, Friedrich Schleiermacher (1768–1834) seems to have been the one who first coined the term 'practical theology'.[7] For him, it was part of his grand effort to rehabilitate Christian faith in the face of what he believed would be its inevitable demise when subjected to rationalistic criticism. He no doubt allowed himself to be unduly influenced by Romanticism, inasmuch as he put religious experience at the centre of things as the essence of Christianity that would remain 'true' even if everything historical or rational was shown to be untrue, though by questioning the dominant cognitive understanding of the nature of theology he was in other respects ahead of his time.[8] He was opposed by those who were wedded to an exclusively rational approach to theology, and denounced for starting to do theology from the wrong end, from human experience rather than from God. In reality, though, he was very constrained by dogma, and what he proposed was essentially a kind of 'applied systematic theology', in which the belief system was primary and 'practical theology' was concerned with asking what the prior belief system might mean if and when it was put into practice. It was not until the 1930s that the concept surfaced again, this time in Scotland, where a reorganization of the Church of Scotland led to its training facilities for ministers being handed over to the ancient Scottish universities of Edinburgh, Glasgow, St Andrews, and Aberdeen, to become the Divinity Schools of those institutions. This gave practical theology a foothold in the academy, though it tended to be very much on the Schleiermacherian model in which the starting point was a question along the lines of 'What does systematic theology look like when it is put into practice?' Not surprisingly, there was not much enthusiasm for this among the academic community, and practical theology remained very much the poor relation of core theological subjects such as biblical studies, ecclesiastical history, philosophy of religion, and systematic theology. My own initial theological training took place in such a context, and it was widely believed among students at the time that the easiest way to get a first-class degree was by specializing in practical theology. It is not hard to see why. For, despite its claims, this way of looking at things really had no secure theological base from which to operate, which meant that practical theologians tended to deal in second-hand concepts whose terms of reference had been previously defined by other specialists. As a consequence, it often amounted to little more than handy tips for ordinands, offering advice on such matters as pastoral visiting and conduct of the occasional offices – all of which clergy need to know, but which hardly requires any particular insight or intellectual effort. For those who wonder, I did not at that time take the easy option by specializing in practical theology, but chose biblical studies – which was presumably not as difficult as it was rumoured to be, as I still got my first-class degree!

Since those days, things have changed a lot and (largely under American influence this time) there is a definite trend towards a more holistic understanding of the nature of practical theology – and, therefore, of theology more generally – which is taking it back towards the sort of incarnational understanding offered in the opening paragraphs of this chapter. Several factors are playing a part in this, among which we might mention four in particular.

A general disillusionment with exclusively rational practices

The reductionist approach encapsulated by Newtonian physics and Cartesian ontology has now played itself out, as we can see that the attempt to rationalize things has not only failed to improve human life, but in some crucial respects has actually made things worse, for all the reasons noted in a previous chapter. If all truth is connected to God, then we have no reason to suppose that a methodology now discredited in relation to other aspects of life will still have validity in theological discourse. In relation to matters of faith, not only is the Cartesian ideal of the autonomous rational individual an un-achievable myth, but we can now see that even if it were possible for us to be that detached person, we would forfeit a significant part of our humanity in the process. Who we truly are involves emotions, relationships, and other embodied experiences, as well as our rational processes. Therefore, to engage anything less than our whole person in the spiritual search will, to one degree or another, be limiting, if not self-defeating. Far from excluding our own per-sonalities and commitments as illegitimate parts of the process of theological reflection, we should begin from who we are, who we wish to be, who we are becoming. Our baggage is not a liability, but can become a key asset in the search for truth. This is not rocket science, but it sometimes takes scholars a long time to figure out what to ordinary people can seem very obvious.

New scientific perspectives

On the Cartesian model, empirical evidence and 'scientific' evidence were assumed to be one and the same thing. Anything that might be worth knowing would always be susceptible of the sort of proof that might be gathered in a laboratory through the due process of careful testing of hypotheses. The manifest inability of this way of working – not to mention Einstein's theories which challenged what had been some fundamental assumptions on the nature of reality – encour-aged the development of a more holistic view of things even in the disciplines of hard science, spurred on by the opening of new hor-izons in astronomy and space exploration. On the one hand, this has led to a more expansive worldview, and on the other to a reassess-ment of what can be allowed as empirical evidence. It is now widely accepted that human experience can be just as empirical as the kind of abstract information generated through detached reasoning.

The next Christendom

The term was coined by Philip Jenkins, and is a short-hand way of describing the massive shift in the centre of gravity of world Christianity that has occurred over the last 50 years or so.[9] Mid-twentieth-century Christianity was still to a large extent the faith of people in the Global North, whereas today the majority of all Christians are in the Global South. Moreover, increasing numbers of them belong to indigenous churches that have no intrinsic connection with historic Christianity in its European manifestations. Many belong to the Pentecostal wing of the Church, something that was in its infancy only a hundred years ago but which now constitutes a fourth major branch of Christianity, alongside the Orthodox, Roman Catholics, and Protestants. The fact that it has infiltrated the other categories through the influence of the charismatic renewal movement only serves to highlight its significance. Two aspects of these trends are challenging traditional ways of understanding the theological enterprise. The first emerged as far back as the 1960s with the growth of base communities among existing colonial churches, especially in South America. This brought a fresh appreciation of the fact that many things – theology included – are bound to look different, depending on an individual's starting point. The idea of the rational autonomous individual makes little sense to those who are poor and illiterate. In that context, there are only two kinds of resource available for doing theology: your own life situation, and your experience of God. This was the starting point for people like Gustavo Gutiérrez, who has been aptly described as the 'father' of liberation theology.[10] He, and others like him, had been sent to Europe to be trained in the methods of traditional theological scholarship, but as they looked for materials that might serve them well in the context of the realities of life in other parts of the world, they came to the realization that there was just one thing that they and the semi-literate people among whom they ministered had in common, and that was the stories of the Bible. As a consequence, liberation theology was a dynamic, person-centred enterprise right from the start, and the key question (the only one that made sense) became, 'What does the Bible look like through the eyes of the poor?' Since then, of course, many others have asked their own parallel questions in other social contexts. The other new ingredient in the mixture is the rapid worldwide growth of Pentecostalism, which in recent years has engendered the emergence of a distinctively

Pentecostal way of doing theology, even among those who by other definitions might be regarded as traditional Western theologians. The literature is growing rapidly, as those whose own spiritual journey coincides with the Pentecostal experience strive to reflect on it and place it in relationship to the traditional methods of the inherited theological paradigm, which by definition excluded experience as unreliable and non-scientific.[11] Though it is too early to be sure of this, it may be that the rise of the emerging church within the mainline denominations of the Global North will add another perspective. For though the emerging church is not generally Pentecostal or charismatic (and in some places is populated by refugees from those churches), it is nevertheless posing some equally fundamental questions regarding what theology actually is, and therefore how we might do it. Since all these non-classical ways of being church are growing, while the traditional mainline denominations are at best static (though mostly declining), it is only natural to wonder if there might be some intrinsic connection between growth and decline and these different ways of doing theology. The least that can be said is that inherited paradigms of theology seem incapable of addressing the decline that is now endemic in churches of the Global North. But there may be a bigger challenge than that: could it be that our traditional understanding of what theology is has actually contributed to the alienation of large sections of the population from the life of the Church?

New questions

Compared with some of the really big questions of the day, all that might count as little more than introspective navel-gazing. Globalization is opening up new vistas of imagination to all the world's peoples, and inherited religious frameworks are being questioned as never before as the adherents of different faith communities meet face to face in ways that would not have been thought possible even a couple of generations ago. Adherents of many faiths are being required to accept the fact that what they once regarded as unique and unquestionable may be just one part of a much bigger jigsaw puzzle that is the world and its spirituality. Some (of all world faiths) find themselves reaffirming traditional beliefs and seeking to impose them on others by whatever means may be possible, though others are wondering if the cause of truth may not be better served by some radical reimagination of all faith traditions. Beyond that, however, an even bigger question is highlighted by the realization that environmental pollution and degradation is going to affect the lifestyles of us all, and may threaten the future thriving of the planet itself. This is another issue that challenges the way theology has been done, if only because the wilful exploitation of the earth's resources has often been justified as being part of God's plan for humankind. Similar awkward questions arise in relation to matters such as racism and sexism, while advances in medical technology continue to present new questions about the meaning of human life itself in relation to matters such as people being kept artificially 'alive' though in a permanent vegetative state – not to mention debates on abortion, euthanasia, and the question of what constitutes disability. If all things cohere in God, then how does any of this connect with the sort of topics with which theologians have hitherto been concerned?

Starting points

Reflecting on that sort of question takes us back to the first chapter of this book, and what was said about the nature of contemporary culture in the Global North. I suggested there that neither 'post-modernity' nor any other cognate term constitutes an all-encompassing coherent worldview in terms of the internal rationality that would historically have been expected of any opinion claiming to give an account of the meaning of life. But that is only half the story, because it would also be widely assumed today that the search for something coherent is itself a waste of time, and that fragmentation, discontinuity, and ultimately meaninglessness, are just part and parcel of the predicament that is our human existence. It no longer bothers people when nothing seems to make sense by the standards of rational understanding. Given that traditional ways of doing theology are founded on a totally different premise (that there is a rational, if not logical, relationship of cause and effect operating in all aspects of human life), it is inevitable that we should have to look for new ways of engaging with the culture if the Christian voice is to be heard as anything other than an outmoded hangover from the past that knows the answers to all the questions that nobody is actually asking. In commending such a fresh approach (which he also identifies as 'practical theology' as distinct from 'applied theology'), Martyn Percy recommends that we learn to 'higgle' (an old English agricultural word meaning to 'affect things by degrees'), to 'thole' ('an old Irish word that describes the process of survival under adverse conditions'), and 'to be engaged in renewal', something he defines as 'a process of recovery and restoration' but also 'replacement', because 'The Christian tradition must face the present and the future, but it cannot neglect its past.'[12] What I am commending here is certainly a different way of doing theology, but a way that will value and draw from the inherited Christian tradition – including the Bible, history, systematic theology, and so on – rather than discarding the accumulated wisdom of centuries. The use of the term 'wisdom' here is intentional, because it connects with the emphasis on lifestyle as an entry point into Christian faith that was explored in some detail in Chapter 3. In that context, I highlighted the growing relevance of the Wisdom Literature of the Hebrew Scriptures in relation to the concerns of today's people to find an appropriate way of living in harmony with the cosmos, with other people, with oneself, and with God. In order for Christian theology to be appropriately contextualized in the culture of the twenty-first century, we need a 'wisdom' way of doing it that will be significantly different from the cognitive mode in which it was contextualized in previous generations, while not dismissing uncritically the insights of those who have gone before us. In the chapter on mission, I highlighted the importance of having due regard to the different entry points through which individuals might come to faith, and the notion of entry points is also relevant here. The following diagram illustrates this:

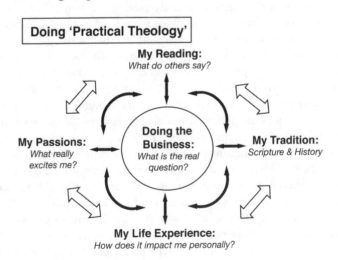

The inherited entry point for theological reflection begins with what is called here 'my tradition', that is with Scripture and its interpretation, which by definition also includes aspects of the history of the Church. Different ecclesiastical and theological traditions might offer distinctive opinions on the precise relationship between these things, but there would be general agreement on their importance for understanding and articulating Christian belief. In practice, much that passes for traditional theology does not in fact start here, but with wider reading, whether through the theories of philosophers or scientists, or in books about the Bible and Church history. I once worked in a university Department of Religious Studies that was entirely secular (even, on occasion, atheistic), where I taught the New Testament and other related aspects of Christian studies. I also have experience of life in traditional departments of Christian theology. Though generalizations never tell the whole story, the students I encountered in the Religious Studies programme were on the whole far more likely to take the Bible seriously by actually reading and wrestling with the text for themselves than were those I have met in theology departments, who (because they were mostly Christians) assumed that they intuitively knew what it was about, so did not need to read it but instead busied themselves finding out what others had to say about it. I remember teaching a New Testament course to seminary students in the USA, and including a test of the contents of its books as part of their assessed work. Not only were they all terrified when the day for the test came around, but my expectation that they should actually read the texts they were supposed to be studying was the talk of the whole institution, as even professors were surprised that I would do such a thing. I suspect that it is eminently possible to get a degree in theology without ever reading the core scriptural texts in any deep way. One of the things I learned from my experience in a Religious Studies context was a realization that even in ostensibly secular contexts, students are looking for some insights into the deep questions of meaning and purpose for their lives, and teachers do them a disservice when they avoid confronting such matters head-on. Paradoxically, this is the one thing to which institutions can be most resistant. In one place where I worked, I remember having fierce arguments with my line managers on this very point, and being left in no doubt that in a modern university this should play no part in any sort of educational agenda, whether related to theology or other subjects. At the same time as those arguments were going on, I happened to be teaching courses that were doing just that, by offering opportunities to reflect on one's own spirituality, and to see it nurtured and developed in whatever ways might be appropriate to an individual's particular circumstances. Needless to say, they were among the most over-subscribed courses in the entire curriculum – and the first to be axed as soon as I resigned from that particular institution. I am not the only one to have come across this phenomenon. Martyn Percy claims that as presently conceived, a primary purpose of theological education is 'to inform, support and consolidate tradition – but not to change it', and I agree with him when he further points out that this is a 'betrayal of the Christian tradition itself and a failure of nerve in the field of theology'.[13] Moreover, this is not some maverick opinion. Richard Lischer is another one who identifies a similar trend as he observes that

> much of what has been passing for theology does not draw its
> life from the gospel and is therefore utterly incapable of
> transforming lives or teaching and leading the church.[14]

Part of the reason for this is that, as with everything else in life, we only commit ourselves to what really excites us, which is one of the other entry points in the diagram ('my passions'). A major reason why so many Christians are disillusioned with what they know of theology is because they have either never known or have lost a sense of passion about the core truths of their own faith. Ultimately, though, not even passion is enough, and most of us make most of our major decisions in life on the basis of how we feel and the way that a particular thing impacts us personally. Our entry point into theological reflection is no different, hence the importance of what on the diagram is labelled 'personal experience'.[15] Given the importance of practical everyday living as an entry point into discipleship for so many people today, we do ourselves (and the Gospel) no favours by relegating it to a minor position as 'a side dish to the main course of true intelligence'.[16]

By isolating these elements in this way, I do not mean to give the impression that some are more important than others. We need them all, and any of them can be a valid starting point for doing theology, and the entry point for each individual will depend on many variables within our own understanding, of ourselves as well as of the wider world and of God. Until recently, however, only two portals have been regarded as approved starting points, namely the one I have labelled 'my tradition', and the other I have called 'my reading'. 'My passions' have been influential behind the scenes, as it were, because no one engages with any sort of topic without feeling passionately about it. And, under the influence of Cartesian notions of disconnected, disembodied rationality, 'my life experience' has been almost entirely excluded from consideration as being irrelevant, unscientific, and quite possibly misleading and dangerous. In the context of twenty-first-century culture, this is a major omission that has direct negative repercussions for the ministry and mission of the Church, a claim that I trust needs no further justification in light of what has already been said along these lines in previous chapters.[17] It is also worth noting, however, that the denial (or even the ignoring) of a relational aspect to the doing of theology not only contradicts the biblical roots of the term itself, but also stands in contrast to the very first page of the Bible, where we are assured that to be human is to be 'made in the image of God' (Gen. 1:27), which seems to imply that if we exclude our own experience of life from the theological enterprise, we might be missing one of the most important components of all. One can think of many reasons for this state of affairs. History and intellectual fads and fashions clearly play a part. So does personality type. As far as I know, no one has ever carried out empirical research into the dominant personality types among academic theologians, but my experience of them over a period of many years suggests that very many are private, introverted individuals who would find it difficult to acknowledge the existence of their own inner life, let alone to share anything of it with another person, and still less to reflect on it in a public sort of way. That alone would be a powerful inbuilt incentive for the prioritizing of tradition and reading over against experience and enthusiasm. There may also be an element of élitism at work as well, for if personal experience is acknowledged to be a valid entry point into the doing of theology, then everybody has their experience, including those who will never cross the threshold of a college or university.

Teaching and learning

Taking all this seriously will obviously have an impact not only on what we think theology is, and how we might do it, but also on how we might learn it not just in the context of the sort of formal theological education that is offered to future ministers of the Gospel, but also in the Christian education programme of the local church.

Having spent most of my life involved in this enterprise, in both contexts, I need to declare a personal interest in securing a meaningful future for college and seminary education, as well as acknowledging that my own story is bound to inform (and quite likely skew) my perceptions of what may now need to be done in order to meet the challenges in mission and ministry identified in earlier chapters of this book. Like many of the topics covered in this book, this is another one that could easily justify an entire volume to itself, and I am conscious that what can be said here is going to be somewhat random and certainly will only touch on a few general principles. I have, however, written in greater detail about some aspects of this subject in my earlier book, *Cultural Change and Biblical Faith*, and readers who want to understand the broader context of my remarks here will find some useful background there.[18]

The idea that authentic theological reflection might start from one's own experience of life and of faith is hardly revolutionary from an educational perspective, as it is now widely recognized that 'there can be no learning that does not begin with experience'.[19] Writing more specifically about the nature of theology, Jeff Astley has argued that 'theology is process as well as content', which is just a different way of saying the same thing.[20] Part of the problem with the typical curriculum that now presents itself as theological education is that it has become disconnected from any deep spiritual process, and consequently reflects a somewhat attenuated version of what theology might actually be. My experience suggests that this limitation runs as a deep fault-line through much of the system, whether in relation to the privatized personalities of many academics or the default position in most theological disciplines that ensures that the main purpose of study will be knowledge of other people's ideas about theology, rather than any living encounter with the divine. Even Don Cupitt – whose major claim to fame is as a self-confessed Anglican atheist – highlights the hollowness of this approach, describing it as a method

> that ensures it is never going to make the slightest difference either to your life or to anyone else's … You don't learn to be a performer; you learn how to be a good critic of other people's performances.[21]

Yet this way of doing theology is deeply entrenched in the system, in theological colleges and seminaries as well as in universities. In the UK, the future viability of entire university faculties depends on points awarded in the government-sponsored Research Assessment Exercise, which imposes a demand for continual publication on academics that leaves insufficient time for the development of truly original ideas, and ensures that most will opt for a style of scholarship that majors on recycling amended versions of other people's ideas. The prevailing climate of McDonaldized outputs means that this kind of cloned theology is also more likely to result in personal promotion than original work which challenges the *status quo* – so who can blame them?

In parallel with this, a false sense of personal freedom means that not only is the study of theology reduced to a study of theologians, but the life-changing potential of encounter with God is either marginalized or excluded. Even in places where spiritual nurture features among the stated aims of theological education, that objective tends to be pursued independently of the ways in which core theological subjects are actually studied, with much of the responsibility for personal formation being assumed to take place through chapel services or other activities that are not a part of the formal accredited programme of learning. In researching material for a contribution to another book, I was astonished to discover that there seems to be no foundational theology course anywhere in the UK that includes homiletics as a core subject in its primary accredited degree courses, even though preaching is a major aspect of ministry in every Christian denomination.[22]

I do not wish to sound too negative here, so I must reaffirm that I see an appropriate and relevant form of theological education having a vital role to play in helping Christians to address the issues of mission and ministry highlighted in previous chapters here. The issue is the proverbial glass of water, that is both half full and half empty. In *The McDonaldization of the Church*, I argued that one of our problems is that we have utilized a limited tool-kit in the past that prioritized cognitive reflection over against creativity, imagination, the arts, and affective spirituality. It is not that the one is right and the other wrong, rather that different circumstances call forth different needs and opportunities. In the chapter on mission, I used the image of a jazz band to suggest that different aspects of the Gospel come to the fore to address different questions, and that just because a particular aspect is not centre stage at any given moment in time does not mean it is less important than those that are. The same image can be applied here in thinking about what it is useful for today's church leaders to know, and in the context of contemporary culture the two axes that are most important are an ability to tell the Christian story (for which biblical studies will be central), and an understanding of how to value the lived experience of people as it informs and inspires their spiritual aspirations (and for that, practical theology as I have defined it here will be the starting point). It is not that other ways of looking at Christian faith are inadmissible, but those which in the past were centre stage may now be more useful in a supporting role, supplying the infrastructure rather than the superstructure.

Style and relationality

Two themes are intertwined here: style (by which I mean the ways in which we do things), and relationality (by which I mean the attitudes with which we do them). In Chapter 2, mention was made of Daniel Pink's claim that the sort of people who will make a difference in what he calls the Conceptual Age are 'creators and empathizers, pattern recognizers, and meaning makers ... artists, storytellers, caregivers, consolers, big picture thinkers'.[23] Others associate these qualities with 'the creative class', individuals who are looking for

> changes in values, your fundamental life priorities; changes in lifestyle, the way you spend your time and money; and changes in livelihood, how you make that money in the first place.[24]

There are several reasons for reflecting on this in relation to how we teach and learn about Christian faith. For one thing, these aspirations reflect much that can be identified with both the message and the style of Jesus as presented in the Gospels. For another, a sizeable percentage of the population is attracted to this: Paul Ray and Sherry Ruth Anderson quote American and European Union statistics to show that cultural creatives now account for roughly a quarter of the population on both continents.[25] Moreover, as I suggested in an earlier chapter, there is a clear correlation between creative-class people, urban tribes, and those I call the spiritual searchers, who are most open to responding to the Gospel and committing themselves to radical discipleship. The characteristic concerns of such individuals therefore offer a checklist for Christian education that could make a significant difference not only in colleges and seminaries but also in local congregations, for they highlight a style of being and learning that will also be missional and transformative, thereby becoming educational in the fully-rounded sense of touching the human person in all its multifaceted complexity.

One thing on which all researchers are agreed is that creative-class people will run a mile from anything that smacks of inauthenticity. They expect – of themselves and of others – that what we do should be consistent with what we say we believe. Their basis of knowing 'involves direct personal experience in addition to intellectual ways'.[26] This challenge to 'walk the talk' is a big one for any Christian, but it is particularly important that those who aspire to teach others should exemplify it. It is an easy matter to proclaim the values of the Gospel, to speak of loving God and neighbour, but a more challenging thing to put it into practice. It is even easier to write books about it than it is to preach sermons on the theme, for readers very rarely know enough about even their favourite authors to be able to call their bluff and highlight their inconsistencies. Most of us learn best from teachers who have integrity, and it is a well-established fact that what teachers are like, to a very large degree impacts what their students become, as we learn not just information but virtues, spirituality, and – in the most comprehensive sense of the word – wisdom. In my own formative theological education, I was fortunate to be mentored by William Lillie – a scholar of a previous generation whose name is unlikely to be known to more than a tiny minority of readers of this book, if indeed to any at all. He was not a famous person, even in his own day. But what he lacked in status, he more than compensated for in spiritual insight. He was an old man in his late sixties by the time I met him. Having spent most of his life working in India, he had the same sort of perspective on theology as a more widely known church leader of a slightly younger generation, Lesslie Newbigin, and though his primary specialism was in biblical studies, he never allowed study of the Scriptures to be limited to textual or historical matters. For him, the way we used the Bible was to be determined by an understanding of global culture and what at the time were new opportunities for constructive mission. He spoke of God being at work in the lives of people well beyond the boundaries of the Church, and emphasized the need for humility in sharing our faith with others, recognizing that God would always be ahead of and beyond us. In his personal demeanour, he embodied that of which he spoke, which is why I still remember him fondly and occasionally wonder who I might have become had I not been nurtured as a young student by one so thoroughly committed to a biblically grounded missional perspective on life. By way of contrast, I reflect on another professor with whom I had dealings more recently, far more intellectually erudite than William Lillie, and author of numerous books on the importance of friendship as a key Christian virtue, but who has to be one of the most devious and deceitful individuals I have ever met, quite incapable of either creating or sustaining meaningful friendship at any level. When those of us who are theological educators complain – as we frequently do – of the state of the churches we serve, could it just be that at least part of the blame for that lies at our own door? Our students – in church and academy – learn at least as much from who we are as they do from what we say. In fact, as Jeff Astley comments, 'Such a learning of character is surely key to any convincing account of Christian learning.'[27] All that, of course, is as relevant to the life of the local church as it is to the academy.

A second mark of cultural creatives is what Ray and Anderson call 'engaged action and whole process learning', something they describe as 'intimate, engaged knowledge that is imbued with the rich, visceral, sensory stuff of life'. Put simply, because linear, analytical thinking no longer works in today's complex world, cultural creatives tend to search for more holistic learning experiences.[28] This is an even bigger challenge, because though pedagogical theorists emphasize the importance of learning that engages all the senses – and in spite of Jesus' recommendation that discipleship should be similarly all-encompassing (Mark 12:28–34) – we have few models to inform our practice here in relation to theology. There has been more creative exploration in the local church context, through projects such as Jerome Berryman's 'Godly Play',[29] than in the academy, where Walter Wink is virtually the only significant scholar brave enough to have published anything along these lines.[30] An aphorism attributed to Albert Einstein observes that 'imagination is more important than knowledge', something that he explained by pointing out that 'knowledge is limited to all we now know and understand, while imagination embraces the entire world, and all there ever will be to know and understand.' In 1994, my wife and I created a course for Fuller Seminary that would embody this approach, and which we entitled 'Spirituality and Creativity for Evangelism and Worship'. We never expected that we would still be teaching it there on a regular basis so many years later, but one of the reasons for its continued popularity is undoubtedly because it combines imagination with knowledge – and fun! From one angle, it can appear to be quite conventional, as we consider topics such as cultural change, hermeneutics, faith development, sermons, and other related themes. But this knowledge component is set within an imaginative framework that not only appeals to students because of its distinctiveness, but also changes the way in which what sound like conventional subjects can be addressed and understood. The course is structured around the concept of a house, with each class consisting of a visit to a different room. We progress from porch to living-room, to kitchen, to garden, to study, to basement, as well as bedroom, bathroom, and other spaces. This is not just a conceptual framework, for our visit to each room incorporates extensive experiential moments that are designed to engage the whole person and which create a safe space in which we can connect the lived reality of our own lives with the bigger cultural context and, ultimately, with the biggest picture of all which is the *missio Dei*. I will resist the temptation to go into more detail here, because students at Fuller Seminary will be reading this and I would not want to spoil the element of surprise for any who might wish to enrol in this class.[31] I will not pretend that it is an easy matter to create learning environments that will facilitate the sort of 'engaged knowledge' that cultural creatives embrace, not least because of the constraints of both time and space within which most churches and seminaries operate. Not only does this sort of learning require a lot more than rooms full of tables and chairs, but it also calls for a more flexible approach to timing, because if we lead others into exploration of what might be challenging corners of their own lives, we must always allow enough time to address in appropriate ways whatever issues might arise. Whenever I am invited to lead workshops in either church or academy, one of the first questions I ask is always about the sort of space that will be available and the timing. Local clergy are just as surprised by this as are college principals – and neither generally know the answer without further research – but these things are crucial because they determine how much imaginative learning might take place.

A third mark of cultural creatives identified by Ray and Anderson concerns the place of women. In student evaluations of the course just mentioned at Fuller Seminary, one of the things consistently highlighted as a major contribution to learning is the fact that this particular course is jointly taught by my wife and myself. The reasons for that are, in one sense, purely pragmatic, for neither of us would have all the skills necessary to do it alone. The notion that women and men can work collaboratively, and on an equal footing without one or other dominating, just seems common sense to me, but the high praise that is heaped upon us for doing what comes naturally has alerted me to the fact that this is still a big issue in many Christian circles. More recently, we have been preaching sermons together in settings as diverse as cathedral worship and struggling small churches, and with the same response. Ten or fifteen years ago I would have assumed that, for most churches, this question of women and men in ministry together had been addressed and dealt with. I have come to realize that at many practical levels this is far from being the case. A couple of years ago my wife and I were invited to consider the possibility of serving as joint ministers in a particular local church. In many ways we were ideally suited to the situation, and could certainly have made a significant contribution to Christian witness in the town in question. Though they were open enough to initiate the conversation, it eventually became clear that too many people in this particular congregation had issues with women in ministry, even if (as in this case) it was in partnership with a man. They could, however, have coped with a woman being designated a 'pastoral assistant', which to me seemed to offer a simple solution: give both of us that title, and in one neat move we could deal with the church's hang-ups and cover our desire to work as equals. That course of action turned out to be more challenging than what, for them, was the bigger issue of women in ministry! There can only be one possible explanation for such attitudes: prejudice. In a recent essay, Jean Mayland (herself an ordained Church of England priest) highlights a different form of the same thing:

> Evangelical members of General Synod now claim that biblical rules about the headship of men in marriage actually apply to the whole of life, and society is wicked to give women equality. Young evangelical women claim the right to practise 'loving subservience to the sacrificial leadership of men'!!!! I have also been devastated by the attitude of many of the younger women priests in the Church of England. They are as bossy, traditional and as authoritarian as any man.[32]

She is not the only one. Martyn Percy notes that 'The pressure to marginalize the feminine is almost irresistible within some ecclesial communities', and connects this with the defensiveness expressed by many whenever practical theologians seek to broaden the base of theological enquiry and understanding beyond the boundaries of what is conventional and cognitive:

> At times, it feels as though the very existence of the church depends on maintaining a dualism between thinking and *feeling*, as though what is felt, sensed and expressed would undermine the ordered hierarchies of truth and those that protect them.[33]

This is one of those subjects that people outside the Church cannot fathom, which is why – regardless of what some might claim – this is not a matter of internal Church politics, but a central mission issue because it is a stumbling-block for some who might otherwise find themselves attracted to the Gospel. According to Callum Brown, it is a major underlying cause of the demise of churchgoing in the UK, because 'There is no longer any femininity or moral identity for [younger women] to seek or affirm at the British Christian church.'[34] Cultural creatives are not just concerned that women should be included, but that what are regarded as women's ways of doing things ought to be valued and affirmed. They typically describe this in terms of:

> feeling empathy and sympathy for others, taking the viewpoint of the one who speaks, seeing personal experiences and first-person stories as important ways of learning, and embracing an ethic of caring.[35]

There is more than an echo in there of the example given to us by Jesus.

In explaining the significance of the creative classes, Paul Ray and Sherry Ruth Anderson observe that 'movements begin when people refuse to live divided lives.'[36] This concern for holistic living displays itself not only in redefined relationships between women and men, but also in an awareness of the importance of 'whole systems ... synthesizing from very disparate, fragmented pieces of information'.[37] To take this seriously in the world of theological learning and Christian education would require a radical rewriting of much that we think we know, not least of which would be the challenge to break down the barriers between different aspects of what we now think theology is.

Questions like this are already on the agenda of some churches, though the ways in which they are being tackled might not necessarily lead to the best outcomes unless we also revisit our inherited views of what constitutes ministry and calling. For the most part, we still operate with a McDonaldized version of ministry, and the challenge in this regard – as in many other areas of life – is how to move away from a 'one size fits all' mentality without losing the best insights from the past. The inherited patterns have changed little from the days when the parish priest might have been the only educated person in the community, and when it was perfectly possible to be a local minister one day and a university professor the next, because everyone had been trained to be an academic, and practical ministry was seen as the natural outcome of this without the necessity for any further reflection on the cultural context (which, in its turn, was not so very different from the world in which the Bible itself had been written). Given that the Bible was written in Hebrew and Greek, and in cultural contexts from the Stone Age to the Roman empire, there will always be a need for those whose fundamental calling will be to elucidate the significance of Scripture for others whose ministries could be as diverse as liturgy and worship, pastoral care, music, the pioneering of emerging church, and more besides. Because of the monochrome nature of ministry in what was an essentially Christian culture, it used to be assumed that all seminary students might, in principle, be the scholars of the future. But the sort of discontinuous cultural change that is now occurring makes that aspiration unrealistic, not least because it is no longer possible for the average person called into ministry – however bright they may be – to give the amount of time (and therefore, in today's world, financial investment) that would be required to gain competence in things like ancient languages and worldviews. The way we do theology in the future needs to be more collaborative – like ministry itself, recognizing that no one individual can be good at everything. Alongside this, we need to be more open about what we can and cannot do, which in turn is likely to create space for mutual support of one another in which we can share the hope that is within us and encourage one another as servants of Christ. This is not the same thing as the sort of dumbing-down that would end up producing a generation of ministers none of whom are particularly expert at anything, but a recognition that what I have proposed as the two major aspects of contextual theology (biblical studies and practical theology) interact with one another by identifying from a practical angle the sort of questions that we now need to address to the Scriptures, without one approach or the other being deemed to be superior.

What we have at the moment reminds me of the Old Testament story of David and Goliath, in which the inspirational David was ready to fight the giant, but King Saul insisted he should go out to battle dressed in his own suit of armour (1 Sam. 17:38–40). There was nothing actually wrong with Saul's armour: it fitted the king perfectly, and had been used to great effect in many previous successful engagements. Moreover, the offer to give it to David was a way of affirming his future potential as a leader. But Saul failed to understand that what had served him well was unserviceable for the challenge that was facing David at that time. Saul (like many who seek to mentor others) assumed that to be successful David would need to have the same skills and insights as he himself had. But David could see that Saul's armour was not only a poor fit, but crucially it was not flexible enough for the nimbleness that would be required if Goliath was to be defeated. To accomplish his ambition, David certainly needed a weapon, but that too had to be different from the cumbersome equipment used by traditional armies in pitched battles. It was not that David despised conventional methods (there is no evidence that he used a stone and slingshot in any later battles), it was just that for this purpose it was the wrong tool for the job. Today, we might think of recycling the armour instead of abandoning it altogether, and that could be a good note on which to end this chapter: how can we recycle the valuable materials that have come down to us from the past, and reshape them into something that will be more serviceable for the future? Doing that will be a project for a complete book to itself, though I have made a start on some aspects of it in relation to sin and redemption in my small book on *Celebrity Culture*.[38] There will obviously be different ways in which Christian belief will be reimagined in different places around the world, which is why I have deliberately avoided being prescriptive here. But whatever shape our theological reflections take, they will be rooted in the two anchor points of the Bible on the one hand and our contemporary human experience on the other. Or, as Karl Barth put it, we will travel through life with the Bible in one hand and the newspaper in the other, reading the newspaper through the message of the Bible.[39]

NOTES

Preface

1. John Drane, *The McDonaldization of the Church* (London, Darton, Longman & Todd, 2000).
2. Daniel H. Pink, *A Whole New Mind* (New York, Riverhead Books, 2006), p. 130.
3. Olive M. Fleming Drane, *Spirituality to Go. Rituals and Reflections for Everyday Living* (London, Darton, Longman & Todd, 2006).
4. The Mission Theological Advisory Group is a joint initiative of the Church of England and the Global Mission Network. For the outcome of our five-year deliberation that is relevant to the concerns of this book see Anne Richards, *Sense Making Faith* (London, CTBI, 2007) and the website http://www.spiritualjourneys.org.uk

Chapter 1: Culture

1. Michael Frost and Alan Hirsch, *The Shaping of Things to Come: Innovation and Mission for the 21st Century Church* (Peabody MA, Hendrickson, 2003), p. 231.
2. http://www.emergentkiwi.org.nz/archives/my_most_significant_ emerging_and_missional_books.php#more
3. John Drane, 'The Church and the Iron Cage', in George Ritzer (ed.), *McDonaldizaton: the Reader* (Thousand Oaks CA, Pine Forge Press, 2002), pp. 151–7; John Drane, 'From Creeds to Burgers: religious control, spiritual search, and the future of the world', in George Ritzer (ed.), *McDonaldization: The Reader*, 2nd edn (Thousand Oaks CA, Pine Forge Press, 2006), pp. 197–202.
4. John Drane, *Introducing the Old Testament*, 2nd edn (Oxford, Lion, 2000); *Introducing the New Testament*, 2nd edn (Oxford, Lion, 1999); *Introducing the Bible* (Minneapolis, Fortress, 2005).
5. John Drane, *Faith in a Changing Culture* (London, HarperCollins, 1997); *Cultural Change and Biblical Faith* (Carlisle, Paternoster Press, 2000).
6. Throughout this book, I have used the term 'Global North' to denote Europe, North America, Australasia, and other industrialized nations that together form the 'rich North' over against the developing countries of the 'Global South'. When referring to the ideology that informs such countries, however, I have used the more traditional term, 'Western'.

7. Cf. Alan Jamieson, *A Churchless Faith* (London, SPCK, 2002).

8. These calculations are based on figures presented in the annual series, *UKCH Religious Trends*, ed. Peter Brierley (London, Christian Research). See also http://www.christian-research.org.uk/intro.htm

9. http://www.barna.org/FlexPage.aspx?Page=BarnaUpdateNarrow Preview&BarnaUpdateID=267

10. George Barna, *Revolution* (Ventura CA, Barna Research, 2005).

11. See Baylor Institute for Studies of Religion, *American Piety in the 21st Century: New insights to the depth and complexity of religion in the US* (Waco TX, Baylor University, 2006). Available for free download at www.baylor.edu/content/services/document.php/33304.pdf

12. The categories to which I refer are efficiency, calculability, predictability, and control, as identified by George Ritzer, *The McDonaldization of Society* (Thousand Oaks CA, Pine Forge Press, 1993). Though I make several references to this in relation to church life in this book, I am not providing a summary of my thinking on this theme, as it has been articulated more comprehensively in *The McDonaldization of the Church* (London, Darton, Longman & Todd, 2000).

13. John Drane, 'From Creeds to Burgers: religious control, spiritual search, and the future of the world', in James R. Beckford and John Walliss (eds), *Theorising Religion* (Aldershot, Ashgate, 2006), pp. 120–31.

14. Cf. Ziauddin Sardar, *Postmodernism and the Other* (London, Pluto Press, 1998).

15. Hugh Fearnley-Whittingstall, *The River Cottage Meat Book* (London, Hodder & Stoughton, 2004), pp. 12–19.

16. Martyn Percy, *Engaging with Contemporary Culture* (Aldershot, Ashgate, 2005), p. 6.

17. Cf. Peter L. Berger (ed.), *The Desecularization of the World* (Grand Rapids MI, Eerdmans, 1999).

18. For an application of the consequences of this to the way we do theology, see Jeff Astley, *Ordinary Theology* (Aldershot, Ashgate, 2002).

19. Cf. Gordon Lynch, *Understanding Theology and Popular Culture* (Oxford, Blackwell, 2005), pp. 1–19.

20. Percy, *Engaging with Contemporary Culture*, p. 29.

21. George Lings, *Living Proof – a new way of being church?* (Sheffield, Church Army, 1999), p. 13.

22. Cf. Harvey Cox, *Fire from Heaven: The rise of Pentecostal spirituality and the reshaping of religion in the 21st century* (Reading MA, Addison-Wesley, 1995).

23. For discussions of this phenomenon, see (from a Christian perspective) John A. Saliba, *Understanding New Religious Movements* (London, Geoffrey Chapman, 1995) and (from a sociological angle) Bryan Wilson and Jamie Cresswell (eds), *New Religious Movements: Challenge and response* (London, Routledge, 1999); Stephen J. Hunt, *Alternative Religions: A sociological introduction* (Aldershot, Ashgate, 2003), pp. 89–130.

24. Cf. John Drane, *Do Christians Know How to Be Spiritual? The Rise of New Spirituality and the Mission of the Church* (London, Darton, Longman & Todd, 2005), pp. 1–40.

25. Paul Heelas and Linda Woodhead, *The Spiritual Revolution: Why religion is giving way to spirituality* (Oxford, Blackwell, 2005).

26. Shirley Maclaine, *Out on a Limb* (London, Bantam, 1986), p. 198.

27. Dan Brown, *The Da Vinci Code* (New York, Doubleday, 2003).

28. David Hay and Kate Hunt, *Understanding the Spirituality of People who don't go to Church* (Nottingham, University of Nottingham Centre for the Study of Human Relations, 2000).

29. Ritzer, *The McDonaldization of Society*, p. 26.

30. For more on this, see Drane, *Do Christians Know How to Be Spiritual?*, pp. 90–120.

31. Martin Rees, *Our Final Century* (London, Heinemann, 2003), p. 8.

32. For the statistics on all this, see Jean M. Twenge, *Generation Me* (New York, Free Press, 2006), pp. 105–9.

33. Alan J. Roxburgh and Fred Romanuk, *The Missional Leader* (San Francisco, Jossey-Bass, 2006), p. 16.

34. David Martin, *On Secularization: Towards a revised general theory* (Aldershot, Ashgate, 2005), pp. 108–19.

35. Robert L. Gallagher, '"Me and God, we'd be Mates": toward an Aussie contextualized Gospel', in *International Bulletin for Missionary Research*, 30/3 (2006), p. 127. Cf. also M. B. ter Borg, 'Some ideas on wild religion', in *Implicit Religion*, 7 (2004).

36. B. Joseph Pine and James H. Gilmore, *The Experience Economy* (Boston MA, Harvard Business School, 1999), pp. 163–4, 183.

37. Ibid., p. 206.

38. Raymond's themes at those events appeared in his *Isaiah Vision* (Geneva, WCC, 1992) and the monthly letters on evangelism he issued from his desk in Geneva, some of which were published as *Evangelistically Yours* (Geneva, WCC, 1992). My own lectures at these events formed the substance of *Faith in a Changing Culture* (London, HarperCollins, 1997).

39. *Economist*, vol. 353, no. 8151 (31 Dec. 1999), p. 135.

40. Thomas C. Oden, *After Modernity – What?* (Grand Rapids MI, Eerdmans, 1990), p. 51.

41. Jean M. Twenge, *Generation Me* (New York, Free Press, 2006), p. 105.

42. John Shore, *Penguins, Pain and the Whole Shebang* (New York, Seabury Books, 2005), p. 46.

43. John Drane, 'Contemporary culture and the reinvention of sacramental spirituality', in Geoffrey Rowell and Christine Hall (eds), *The Gestures of God: Explorations in sacramentality* (London, Continuum, 2004), pp. 37–55.

Chapter 2: Community

1. Douglas Coupland, *Microserfs* (London, Flamingo, 1995), p. 313.

2. Daniel Pink, *A Whole New Mind* (New York, Riverhead Books, 2006).

3. For more extensive discussion of this, see John Drane and Olive M. Fleming Drane, *Family Fortunes* (London, Darton, Longman & Todd, 2004), pp. 1–41.

4. Jean M. Twenge, *Generation Me* (New York, Free Press, 2006), p. 115.

5. Helen Fielding, *Bridget Jones's Diary* (London, Picador, 1997).

6. http://www.cuddleparty.com

7. Pamela Paul, *The Starter Marriage and the Future of Matrimony* (New York, Random House, 2003); Kate Harrison, *The Starter Marriage: A Novel* (London, Orion, 2005).

8. Peter L. Berger, Brigitte Berger and Hansfried Kellner, *The Homeless Mind: Modernization and Consciousness* (New York, Vintage Books, 1974).

9. Ibid., p. 187.

10. This is not the whole story, of course: cf. John Drane, *Do Christians Know How to Be Spiritual?* (London, Darton, Longman & Todd, 2005), pp. 1–89.

11. For a well-informed theological reflection on this topic, see Eric O. Jacobsen, *Sidewalks in the Kingdom: New Urbanism and the Christian Faith* (Grand Rapids MI, Brazos Press, 2003).

12. UNFPA, *State of World Population 2007: Unleashing the potential of urban growth* (New York, United Nations, 2007).

13. Cf. F. M. L. Thomson, *The Rise of Suburbia* (Leicester, Leicester University Press, 1982); C. M. H. Carr, *Twentieth Century Suburbs* (London, Routledge, 2001).

14. On American suburbs, see Robert Fishman, *Bourgeois Utopias: The rise and fall of suburbia* (New York, Basic Books, 1987); Dolores Hayden, *Building Suburbia: Green Fields and Urban Growth 1820–2000* (New York, Pantheon, 2003).

15. Cf. Alan J. Roxburgh and Fred Romanuk, *The Missional Leader* (San Francisco, Jossey-Bass, 2006), p. 156.

16. See Michel Maffesoli, *The Time of Tribes: Decline of Individualism in Mass Society* (Thousand Oaks CA, Sage, 1995); Ethan Watters, *Urban Tribes* (New York, Bloomsbury, 2003).

17. Berger, Berger and Kellner, *The Homeless Mind*, p. 214.

18. For introductory treatments of emergence theory, see John H. Holland, *Emergence: From Chaos to Order* (Oxford, Oxford University Press, 2000); Steven Johnson, *Emergence: The connected lives of ants, brains, cities, and software* (New York, Penguin, 2001); Richard Pascale, Mark Millemann and Linda Gioja, *Surfing the Edge of Chaos* (New York, Random House, 2001).

19. Watters, *Urban Tribes*, p. 8.

20. Ibid., p. 10.

21. Cf. Robert D. Putnam, *Bowling Alone: The collapse and revival of American community* (New York, Simon & Schuster, 2000).

22. Watters, *Urban Tribes*, p. 38.

23. Stephen Cottrell, *From the Abundance of the Heart: Catholic Evangelism for all Christians* (London, Darton, Longman & Todd, 2006), p. 37.

24. Cf. Richard A. Batey, *Jesus & the Forgotten City: New Light on Sepphoris and the Urban World of Jesus* (Grand Rapids, Baker, 1991).

25. Marion Leach Jacobsen, *Crowded Pews and Lonely People* (Wheaton IL, Tyndale House, 1975), p. 41.

26. John Shore, *Penguins, Pain and the Whole Shebang* (New York, Seabury Books, 2005), p. 69.

27. Cf. William D. Hendricks, *Exit Interviews* (Chicago, Moody Press, 1993); Philip J. Richter and Leslie J. Francis, *Gone but not Forgotten* (London, Darton, Longman & Todd, 1998).

28. Michael Riddell, Mark Pierson and Cathy Kirkpatrick, *The Prodigal Project: Journeying into the emerging church* (London, SPCK, 2000), p. 11.

29. The story is recounted in Olive M. Fleming Drane, *Clowns, Storytellers, Disciples* (Oxford, BRF, 2002), pp. 211–18.

30. Jeff Astley, *Ordinary Theology* (Aldershot, Ashgate, 2002), pp. 36–7.

31. Cf. 1 Cor. 5:1–5; 1 John.

32. Paul Heelas and Linda Woodhead, *The Spiritual Revolution* (Oxford, Blackwell, 2005).

33. Ibid., p. 149.

34. Paul Heelas and Linda Woodhead, 'Homeless minds today?' in Linda Woodhead (ed.), *Peter Berger and the Study of Religion* (London, Routledge, 2002), p. 43.

35. Church of England General Synod, *The Mission-Shaped Church* (London, Church House Publishing, 2004).

36. http://www.freshexpressions.org.uk

37. For a more extensive discussion of this taxonomy, see John Drane, 'Editorial' in *International Journal for the Study of the Christian Church*, 6/1 (2006), pp. 3–11.

38. Kester Brewin, *The Complex Christ: Signs of emergence in the urban church* (London, SPCK, 2004), p. 70.

39. The precise meaning of 'emergent' is itself unclear. It seems to have originated with Americans who are experimenting with new forms of church within a generally fundamentalist–evangelical context, as a way of distancing themselves from the use of the term 'emerging Christianity' (not 'church') by more radical scholars such as Marcus Borg, e.g. in his *Jesus: Uncovering the life, teachings, and relevance of a religious revolutionary* (San Francisco, HarperSanFrancisco, 2006). However, others who are operating in a more global – and theologically diverse – context seem to wish to distance themselves from the word 'emergent' because it has become a commercial brand in the USA, and use of the term 'emerging' is a way of establishing a distinctive identity.

40. D. A. Carson, *Becoming Conversant with the Emerging Church* (Grand Rapids MI, Zondervan, 2005).

41. Cf. Dave Tomlinson, *The Post-Evangelical* (London, Triangle, 1995; revised North American edition: Grand Rapids MI, Zondervan, 2003).

42. Especially Brian D. McLaren, *A New Kind of Christian* (San Francisco,

Jossey-Bass, 2001); see also his *A Generous Orthodoxy* (Grand Rapids MI, Zondervan, 2006).

43. http://www.sanctus1.co.uk

44. Ben Edson, 'An exploration into the missiology of the emerging church in the UK through the narrative of *Sanctus1*', in *International Journal for the Study of the Christian Church*, 6/1 (2006), p. 31.

45. Victor Turner, *The Ritual Process* (Chicago, Aldine, 1969), p. 128.

46. Eddie Gibbs and Ryan Bolger, *Emerging Churches* (Grand Rapids MI, Baker Academic, 2005).

47. For a survey and summary of issues raised by 'the quest for the historical Jesus', see Gregory W. Dawes (ed.), *The Historical Jesus Quest* (Louisville KY, Westminster John Knox Press, 1999); and on the New Testament Gospels as ancient biographies, see Richard A. Burridge, *What are the Gospels?*, 2nd edn (Grand Rapids MI, Eerdmans, 2004); Richard J. Bauckham, *Jesus and the Eyewitnesses* (Grand Rapids MI, Eerdmans, 2006).

48. David J. Bosch, *Transforming Mission* (Maryknoll NY, Orbis, 1991), pp. 389–93.

49. For more on this, see John Drane, 'From Creeds to Burgers: religious control, spiritual search, and the future of the world', in James R. Beckford and John Walliss (eds.), *Theorising Religion* (Aldershot, Ashgate, 2006), pp. 120–31. Also in abridged form in George Ritzer, *McDonaldization: The Reader*, 2nd edn (Thousand Oaks CA, Pine Forge Press, 2006), pp. 197–202.

50. Ray S. Anderson, *The Shape of Practical Theology* (Downers Grove IL, InterVarsity, 2001), p. 104.

51. Ibid., p. 112.

52. For more on this, see John Drane, 'Maturity in the emerging church', in Steven Croft (ed.), *Mission-shaped Questions: Defining issues for today's church* (London, Church House Publishing, 2008), pp. 90-101.

53. An outlook that was based on a misunderstanding of the way in which the notion of 'the world' is used in the New Testament, not to describe culture (which, by itself, is spiritually and ethically neutral) but as a designation for a worldview that was opposed to the fundamental values of the Gospel. See, e.g., Rom. 12:2; Jas. 4:4; and extensively throughout 1 John.

54. Christine D. Pohl, *Making Room: Recovering Hospitality as a Christian Tradition* (Grand Rapids MI, Eerdmans, 1999), p. 171.

55. Douglas Coupland, *Generation X* (London, Abacus, 1992), p. 8.

56. Cf. Robert E. Webber, *Ancient-Future Faith* (Grand Rapids MI, Baker Academic, 1999); *Ancient-Future Evangelism* (Grand Rapids MI, Baker Academic, 2003); *Ancient-Future Time* (Grand Rapids MI, Baker Academic, 2004).

57. Ray S. Anderson, *The Shape of Practical Theology* (Downers Grove IL, InterVarsity, 2001), p. 106.

58. Daniel H. Pink, *A Whole New Mind* (New York, Riverhead Books, 2006), p. 1.
59. Richard Florida, *Cities and the Creative Class* (New York, Routledge, 2005).
60. http://www.inthirdspace.net/main.html
61. http://www.starbucks.com/customer/faq_qanda.asp?name=whitecup. As far as I know, the cups carrying these sayings are not currently in use in every country, but they can all be accessed at http://www.starbucks.com/retail/thewayiseeit_default.asp?cookie%5Ftest=1
62. Sharon Daloz Parks, *Big Questions, Worthy Dreams: mentoring young adults in their search for meaning, purpose and faith* (San Francisco, Jossey-Bass, 2000), p. 128.

Chapter 3: Mission

1. Stephen Cottrell, *From the Abundance of the Heart* (London, Darton, Longman & Todd, 2006), p. xi.
2. This body was superseded in 1990 by *Action of Churches Together in Scotland*, which includes Roman Catholics as full members.
3. Martyn Percy, *Engaging with Contemporary Culture* (Aldershot, Ashgate, 2005), p. 13.
4. On clown ministry, see Olive M. Fleming Drane, *Clowns, Storytellers, Disciples* (Minneapolis MN, Augsburg, 2004).
5. Olive M. Fleming Drane, *Spirituality to Go: Rituals and Reflections for Everyday Living* (London, Darton, Longman & Todd, 2006); John Drane, *The McDonaldization of the Church* (London, Darton, Longman & Todd, 2000); John Drane, *Do Christians Know How to Be Spiritual? The Rise of New Spirituality and the Mission of the Church* (London, Darton, Longman & Todd, 2005).
6. Cf. Stephen Soldz and Leigh McCullough (eds), *Reconciling Empirical Knowledge and Clinical Experience: The Art and Science of Psychotherapy* (Washington DC, American Psychological Association, 1999).
7. Richard Florida, *The Rise of the Creative Class* (New York, Basic Books, 2002); cf. also Paul H. Ray and Sherry Ruth Anderson, *The Cultural Creatives* (New York, Three Rivers Press, 2000).
8. Erik H. Erikson, *Childhood and Society*, 2nd edn (New York, Norton, 1950); *Identity, Youth and Crisis* (New York, Norton, 1968).
9. Walter Ong, *Orality and Literacy* (London, Methuen, 1982), p. 48.
10. For more along these lines, see Jeremy Carrette and Richard King, *Selling Spirituality: The silent takeover of religion* (London, Routledge, 2004).
11. The figures quoted here represent the average for the whole of the UK. There were significant differences between the various nations, with 65% in Scotland claiming to be Christian, and 86% in Northern Ireland. There were also regional variations within England, with only 58% of Londoners being Christian, but 80% in north-east England and 78% in

the north-west. For more detail, see http://www.statistics.gov.uk/focuson/religion/

12. Peter Brierley, *Pulling out of the Nosedive. A contemporary picture of churchgoing: What the 2005 English Church Census reveals* (London, Christian Research, 2006), pp. 12–14.

13. Michael Shermer, 'Atheists are Spiritual too', at http://www.beliefnet.com/story/172/story_17215_1.html

14. Richard Dawkins, *The God Delusion* (London, Bantam Press, 2006).

15. http://www.timesonline.co.uk/tol/comment/faith/article1767506.ece

16. http://www.atheistsforjesus.com

17. On brain science and spirituality, see Andrew Newberg and Eugene D'Aquili, *Why God won't go away: Brain science and the biology of belief* (New York, Ballantine, 2002); Rhawn Joseph (ed.), *Neurotheology: Brain, Science, Spirituality, Religious Experience* (San Jose CA, San Jose University Press, 2003); David Hay, *Something There: The biology of the human spirit* (London, Darton, Longman & Todd, 2006).

18. For extensive discussion of this phenomenon, see Eddie Gibbs, *In Name Only: Tackling the Problem of Nominal Christianity* (Wheaton IL, Bridgepoint, 1994).

19. Cf. Abraham Maslow, *Toward a Psychology of Being*, 2nd edn (New York, Van Nostrand Reinhold, 1968).

20. The USA has always had more of such people than the UK, not least because some of the founders of the nation were interested in these matters, and the major religious faith to have originated in the USA (Mormonism) has a strong core of such belief. According to the Baylor Religion Survey, *American Piety in the 21st Century* (September 2006, available for free download at www.baylor.edu/content/services/document.php/33304.pdf), some 41% of the American public believe that ancient advanced civilizations like Atlantis really existed, while 37% believe places can be haunted, 25% believe that UFOs are spaceships from other worlds, and 18% expect that creatures like Bigfoot and the Loch Ness monster will eventually be discovered. Surprisingly, only 8% of men and 18% of women believe that psychics can really see the future. There has been no comparable research carried out in the UK.

21. Shirley Maclaine, *Out on a Limb* (London, Bantam, 1983).

22. I have connected 'transitional' and 'charismatic' because historically it is possible to trace the emergence of the characteristics of what we now call charismatic Christianity at points of cultural transition, whether that be the American War of Independence (correlating with the Great Awakening), the move to the West in the USA (coinciding with the rise of classic Pentecostalism), the aftermath of World War I (the emergence of Pentecostalism in the UK), or the cultural traumas of the 1960s (accompanied by the rise of the charismatic movement in many ecclesiastical traditions). The effort now to reconnect charismatic Christianity with roots in the ancient Church, both East and West, may well be

related to the fact that the cultural transition that brought it to birth at the end of the twentieth century is now well established. For an example of the effort to create a new identity for charismatic churches, see Andrew Walker and Luke Bretherton, *Remembering our Future* (London, Paternoster Press, 2007), in which various authors seek to incorporate liturgies and theologies from the wider Church into their own charismatic context – something that seems to be a contradiction in terms because the charismatic movement to a very large extent (especially in its independent form) intrinsically involved a firm rejection of the very things that are now being reclaimed.

23. See, e.g., http://news.bbc.co.uk/2/hi/programmes/newsnight/4071 805.stm

24. See Fergus Macdonald, *The Psalms and Spirituality: A Study of Meditative Engagement with Selected Psalms among Edinburgh Students* (PhD thesis, University of Edinburgh, 2007).

25. For more on this, see John Drane, *Faith in a Changing Culture* (London, HarperCollins, 1997), pp. 218–23; Richard V. Peace, *Conversion in the New Testament* (Grand Rapids MI, Eerdmans, 1999).

26. Richard Rohr, *Simplicity: The art of living* (New York, Crossroad, 1991), p. 59.

27. James Fowler, *Stages of Faith: The psychology of human development and the quest for meaning* (San Francisco, Harper & Row, 1981); John H. Westerhoff III, *Will our Children have Faith?*, 2nd edn (Harrisburg PA, Morehouse, 2000).

28. C. S. Lewis, *Surprised by Joy: The shape of my early life* (London, Geoffrey Bles, 1955), pp. 28–9.

29. Readers familiar with the work of Raymond Fung will recognize some similarities between what I am proposing here in relation to lifestyle and his notion of 'The Isaiah Vision' as a key to effective mission. Cf. Raymond Fung, *The Isaiah Vision* (Geneva, WCC, 1992).

30. Stuart Murray, *Post-Christendom* (Carlisle, Paternoster Press, 2004), p. 203.

31. For more on revivalism, see Ian Stackhouse, *Gospel Driven Church* (Carlisle, Paternoster Press, 2004), p. 28.

32. Lesslie Newbigin, *The Gospel in a Pluralist Society* (Grand Rapids, Eerdmans, 1992), p. 216.

Chapter 4: Ministry

1. Peter Brierley, *Pulling out of the Nosedive. A contemporary picture of churchgoing: What the 2005 English Church Census reveals* (London, Christian Research, 2006), pp. 153–63.

2. Cf. Philip B. Wilson, *Being Single in the Church Today: Insights from History and Personal Stories* (Harrisburg PA, Morehouse, 2005).

3. Alan Jamieson, *A Churchless Faith* (London, SPCK, 2002); Alan Jamieson,

Jenny McIntosh and Adrienne Thompson, *Church Leavers* (London, SPCK, 2006).

4. B. Joseph Pine and James H. Gilmore, *The Experience Economy* (Boston MA, Harvard Business School Press, 1999).

5. For those who will be helped by knowing this, I should point out that Pine and Gilmore are both Christians, which no doubt explains their use of biblical models that I mentioned in Chapter 1, and the dedication of their book: 'To the Author and Perfecter of our faith'.

6. Pine and Gilmore, *The Experience Economy*, p. 192.

7. Ibid., p. 194.

8. Kevin Treston, *Creative Christian Leadership* (Mystic CT, Twenty-Third Publications, 2000).

9. Richard Higginson, *Transforming Leadership* (London, SPCK, 1996).

10. Associated with the work of Donald A. McGavran, *Understanding Church Growth* (Grand Rapids MI, Eerdmans, 1970).

11. On which, see G. A. Pritchard, *Willow Creek seeker services: Evaluating a new way of doing church* (Grand Rapids MI, Baker, 1996). More recently, Willow Creek church itself has had to come to terms with the limited possibilities offered by the 'seeker friendly' model of church, and has identified some of the same issues I have highlighted as being key to the spiritual nurture of today's converts. Cf Greg Hawkins and Cally Parkinson, *Reveal* (Barrington IL, Willow Creek Association, 2007); see also the website http://www.revealnow.com

12. François Lyotard, *The Postmodern Condition* (Minneapolis MN, University of Minnesota Press, 1993), p. xxiv.

13. Alan J. Roxburgh and Fred Romanuk, *The Missional Leader* (San Francisco, Jossey-Bass, 2006), pp. 86–7.

14. Kenneth Schuman and Ronald Paxton, *The Michelangelo Method* (New York, McGraw-Hill, 2006). See also http://www.michelangelomethod.com/

15. David Buttrick, *Preaching Jesus Christ: An exercise in homiletic theology* (Minneapolis MN, Fortress Press, 1988), p. 48.

16. Richard Bewes, 'The Preaching that cannot stop', in *Decision Magazine*, 50 (Sept./Oct. 2005), p. 21.

17. Dan Brown, *The Da Vinci Code* (New York, Doubleday, 2003).

18. For a comprehensive analysis of the Alpha course, see Andrew Brookes (ed.), *The Alpha Phenomenon: Theology, praxis and challenges for mission and church today* (London, CTBI, 2007).

19. For a practical reflection on how this might be accomplished, cf. Alan Kreider, 'Baptism and Catechesis as spiritual formation' in Andrew Walker and Luke Bretherton (eds), *Remembering our Future: Explorations in Deep Church* (London, Paternoster Press, 2007), pp. 170–206.

Chapter 5: Theology

1. Cf. Richard Dawkins, *The God Delusion* (London, Bantam, 2006); Christopher Hitchens, *God is not Great: The case against Religion* (London, Atlantic Books, 2007).

2. For those unfamiliar with colloquial usage, 'gay' once meant 'happy' but now means 'homosexual'; 'cool' used to mean (and still does in some contexts) of a low temperature, but is frequently used to mean 'trendy'; and 'wicked' (originally meaning something exceedingly bad in a moral sense) is now used to mean something good, exciting, and desirable.

3. Philo, *De Praemiis et Poenis*, 53.

4. For more on the style that I think characterizes both of them, see John Drane, 'Patterns of Evangelization in Paul and Jesus: a way forward in the Jesus-Paul debate?' in Joel B. Green and Max Turner (eds), *Jesus of Nazareth: Lord and Christ* (Grand Rapids MI, Eerdmans, 1994), pp. 281–96.

5. Jeff Astley, *Ordinary Theology* (Aldershot, Ashgate, 2002), p. 1.

6. Interview with Catherine Pepinster, discussing his TV series *The Story of God*. Reported at http://www.thetablet.co.uk/cgi-bin/archive_db.cgi/tablet-01117

7. F. D. E. Schleiermacher, *Die Praktische Theologie* (Berlin, 1850), pp. 27–8.

8. Cf. his books *On Religion: Speeches to its Cultured Despisers* (1799); and *The Christian Faith* (1821).

9. Philip Jenkins, *The Next Christendom*, 2nd edn (New York, Oxford University Press, 2007).

10. See, among many others, his classic work *We Drink from our own Wells: The spiritual journey of a people*, 2nd edn (London, SCM, 2005).

11. Cf. Mark Cartledge, *Practical Theology: Charismatic and Empirical Perspectives* (Carlisle, Paternoster, 2003), and the emergence of series such as *The Pentecostal Commentary*, or the *Journal of Pentecostal Theology* and its *Supplement* series, all published by Continuum, a leading academic publisher.

12. Martyn Percy, *Engaging with Contemporary Culture* (Aldershot, Ashgate, 2005), p. 7.

13. Ibid., p. 91.

14. Richard Lischer, *A Theology of Preaching* (Durham NC, Labyrinth, 1992), p. 4.

15. Astute readers will notice that this diagram, with its various entry points, is similar – though not identical to – the hermeneutical cycle familiar from liberation theology. For a practical example of how personal experience can be an entry point into theological reflection, see Don S. Browning, *A Fundamental Practical Theology* (Minneapolis MN, Fortress Press, 1991).

16. Daniel H. Pink, *A Whole New Mind* (New York, Riverhead Books, 2006), p. 16.

17. On the conversation between Christian tradition, personal experience, and cultural information, see also J. D. Whitehead and E. E. Whitehead, *Method in Ministry* (New York, Seabury Press, 1980).

18. John Drane, *Cultural Change and Biblical Faith* (Carlisle, Paternoster, 2000), pp. 104–53.

19. Peter Jarvis, *Adult and Continuing Education: Theory and Practice* (London, Routledge, 1995), p. 66.

20. Astley, *Ordinary Theology*, p. 56.

21. Don Cupitt, *Philosophy's own Religion* (London, SCM Press, 2000), p. 47.

22. I may have missed something, and if so readers will no doubt be quick to point this out. As far as I can see, there are only two exceptions in the UK, both Master's degrees: one at International Christian College in Glasgow (http://www.icc.ac.uk/courses_desc.php?course_id=26) and the other at Spurgeon's College in London (http://www.spurgeons.ac.uk/site/pages/ui_courses_masters.aspx).

23. Daniel H. Pink, *A Whole New Mind* (New York, Riverhead Books, 2006), p. 1.

24. Paul H. Ray and Sherry Ruth Anderson, *The Cultural Creatives* (New York, Three Rivers Press, 2000), p. 4.

25. Ibid., p. 5.

26. Ibid., p. 8.

27. Astley, *Ordinary Theology*, p. 8.

28. Ray and Anderson, *The Cultural Creatives*, p. 9.

29. Jerome W. Berryman, *Godly Play: A way of religious education* (San Francisco, HarperCollins, 1991); see also http://www.godlyplay.com

30. Walter Wink, *Transforming Bible Study*, 2nd edn (Nashville TN, Abingdon, 1990).

31. For more information, see http://www.fuller.edu/sot/ecds/063/EV509_Drane-Drane.html

32. Jean Mayland, 'The Ordination of Women and the Ecumenical Movement', in Janet Wootton (ed.), *This is Our Story* (Peterborough, Epworth Press, 2007), p. 124.

33. Percy, *Engaging with Contemporary Culture*, p. 113.

34. Callum G. Brown, *The Death of Christian Britain* (London, Routledge, 2001), p. 196.

35. Ray and Anderson, *The Cultural Creatives*, p. 12.

36. Ibid., p. 20.

37. Ibid., p. 11.

38. John Drane, *Celebrity Culture* (Edinburgh, Rutherford House, 2006).

39. A widely quoted aphorism from Karl Barth, though its actual source is much disputed. He evidently said this in an interview reported in *Time* for 31 May 1963. See http://libweb.ptsem.edu/collections/barth/faq/quotes.aspx?menu=296&subText=468

BIBLIOGRAPHY

Ray S. Anderson, *The Shape of Practical Theology* (Downers Grove IL, Inter-Varsity, 2001)

Ray S. Anderson, *An Emergent Theology for Emerging Churches* (Downers Grove IL, InterVarsity, 2006)

Jeff Astley, *Ordinary Theology* (Aldershot, Ashgate, 2002)

George Barna, *Revolution* (Ventura CA, Barna Research, 2005)

Zygmunt Bauman, *Liquid Life* (Boston MA, Polity Press, 2005)

William J. Bausch, *Storytelling Imagination and Faith* (Mystic CT, Twenty-Third Publications, 1984)

Baylor Institute for Studies of Religion, *American Piety in the 21st Century: New insights to the depth and complexity of religion in the US* (Waco TX, Baylor University, 2006)

Peter L. Berger (ed.), *The Desecularization of the World* (Grand Rapids MI, Eerdmans, 1999)

Peter L. Berger, Brigitte Berger and Hansfried Kellner, *The Homeless Mind: Modernization and Consciousness* (New York, Vintage Books, 1974)

Jerome W. Berryman, *Godly Play: A way of religious education* (San Francisco, HarperCollins, 1991)

David J. Bosch, *Transforming Mission* (Maryknoll NY, Orbis, 1991)

Kester Brewin, *The Complex Christ: Signs of emergence in the urban church* (London, SPCK, 2004)

Peter Brierley, *Pulling out of the Nosedive. A contemporary picture of church-going: What the 2005 English Church Census reveals* (London, Christian Research, 2006)

Andrew Brookes (ed.), *The Alpha Phenomenon: Theology, praxis and challenges for mission and church today* (London, CTBI, 2007)

Callum G. Brown, *The Death of Christian Britain* (London, Routledge, 2001)

Rosalind Brown et al., *Spirituality in the City* (London: SPCK 2005)

Don S. Browning, *A Fundamental Practical Theology* (Minneapolis MN, Fortress Press, 1991)

Steve Bruce, *God is Dead: Secularization in the West* (Oxford, Blackwell, 2002)

C. M. H. Carr, *Twentieth Century Suburbs* (London, Routledge, 2001)

Jeremy Carrette and Richard King, *Selling Spirituality: The silent takeover of religion* (London, Routledge, 2004)

Craig A Carter, *Rethinking Christ and Culture: A post-Christendom perspective* (Grand Rapids MI, Brazos Press, 2006)

Mark Cartledge, *Practical Theology: Charismatic and Empirical Perspectives* (Carlisle, Paternoster, 2003)

David Chidester, *Authentic Fakes: Religion and American popular culture* (Los Angeles, University of California Press, 2005)

Church of England General Synod, *The Mission-Shaped Church* (London, Church House Publishing, 2004)

Stephen Cottrell, *From the Abundance of the Heart: Catholic Evangelism for all Christians* (London, Darton, Longman & Todd, 2006)

Harvey Cox, *Fire from Heaven: The rise of Pentecostal spirituality and the reshaping of religion in the 21st century* (Reading MA, Addison-Wesley, 1995)

Steven Croft, *Transforming Communities: Re-imagining the Church for the 21st Century* (London, Darton, Longman & Todd, 2002)

Steven Croft et al., *Evangelism in a Spiritual Age* (London, Church House Publishing, 2005)

Steven Croft (ed.), *Mission-shaped Questions: Defining issues for today's Church* (London, Church House Publishing, 2008)

Don Cupitt, *Philosophy's own Religion* (London, SCM Press, 2000)

Sharon Daloz Parks, *Big Questions, Worthy Dreams: Mentoring young adults in their search for meaning, purpose and faith* (San Francisco, Jossey-Bass, 2000)

Grace Davie, Paul Heelas and Linda Woodhead (eds), *Predicting Religion: Christian, Secular, and Alternative Futures* (Aldershot, Ashgate, 2003)

Craig Detweiler and Barry Taylor, *A Matrix of Meanings* (Grand Rapids MI, Baker Academic, 2003)

John Drane, *Faith in a Changing Culture* (London, HarperCollins, 1997)

John Drane, *Cultural Change and Biblical Faith* (Carlisle, Paternoster Press, 2000)

John Drane, *The McDonaldization of the Church* (London, Darton, Longman & Todd, 2000)

John Drane, 'Contemporary culture and the reinvention of sacramental spirituality', in Geoffrey Rowell and Christine Hall (eds), *The Gestures of God: Explorations in sacramentality* (London, Continuum, 2004), pp. 37–55.

John Drane, *Do Christians Know How to Be Spiritual? The Rise of New Spirituality and the Mission of the Church* (London, Darton, Longman & Todd, 2005)

John Drane, 'From Creeds to Burgers: religious control, spiritual search, and the future of the world', in James R. Beckford and John Walliss (eds), *Theorising Religion* (London, Ashgate, 2006), pp. 120–31. Also in abridged form in George Ritzer, *McDonaldization: The Reader*, 2nd edn (Thousand Oaks CA, Pine Forge Press, 2006), pp. 197–202.

John Drane, *Celebrity Culture* (Edinburgh, Rutherford House, 2006)

John Drane and Olive M. Fleming Drane, *Family Fortunes: Faith-full caring for today's families* (London, Darton, Longman & Todd, 2004)

Erik H. Erikson, *Childhood and Society*, 2nd edn (New York, Norton, 1950)

Erik H. Erikson, *Identity, Youth and Crisis* (New York, Norton, 1968)

Robert Fishman, *Bourgeois Utopias: The rise and fall of suburbia* (New York, Basic Books, 1987)

Kieran Flanagan and Peter C. Jupp (eds), *A Sociology of Spirituality* (Aldershot, Ashgate, 2007)

Olive M. Fleming Drane, *Clowns, Storytellers, Disciples* (Minneapolis MN, Augsburg, 2004)

Olive M. Fleming Drane, *Spirituality to Go. Rituals and Reflections for Everyday Living* (London, Darton, Longman & Todd, 2006)

Richard Florida, *The Rise of the Creative Class* (New York, Basic Books, 2002)

Richard Florida, *Cities and the Creative Class* (New York, Routledge, 2005)

Richard Florida, *The Flight of the Creative Class* (New York, HarperCollins, 2007)

Charles R. Foster, Lisa E. Dahill, Lawrence E. Golemon and Barbara Wang Tolentino, *Educating Clergy* (San Francisco, Jossey-Bass, 2006)

James Fowler, *Stages of Faith: The psychology of human development and the quest for meaning* (San Francisco, Harper & Row, 1981)

Nathan C. P. Frambach, *Emerging Ministry* (Minneapolis MN, Augsburg, 2007)

Michael Frost and Alan Hirsch, *The Shaping of Things to Come: Innovation and Mission for the 21st Century Church* (Peabody MA, Hendrickson, 2003)

Raymond Fung, *The Isaiah Vision* (Geneva, WCC, 1992)

Raymond Fung, *Evangelistically Yours* (Geneva, WCC, 1992)

Eddie Gibbs, *In Name Only: Tackling the Problem of Nominal Christianity* (Wheaton IL, Bridgepoint, 1994)

Eddie Gibbs, *Leadership Next* (Downers Grove IL, InterVarsity Press, 2005)

Eddie Gibbs and Ryan Bolger, *Emerging Churches* (Grand Rapids MI, Baker Academic, 2005)

Timothy K. Gorringe, *A Theology of the Built Environment* (Cambridge, Cambridge University Press, 2002)

Darrell L. Guder (ed.), *Missional Church* (Grand Rapids MI, Eerdmans, 1998)

Douglas J. Hall, *The End of Christendom and the Future of Christianity* (Valley Forge PA, Trinity Press International, 1997)

David Hay and Kate Hunt, *Understanding the Spirituality of People who don't go to Church* (Nottingham, University of Nottingham Centre for the Study of Human Relations, 2000)

David Hay, *Something There: The biology of the human spirit* (London, Darton, Longman & Todd, 2006)

Dolores Hayden, *Building Suburbia: Green Fields and Urban Growth 1820–2000* (New York, Pantheon, 2003)

Paul Heelas and Linda Woodhead, *The Spiritual Revolution: Why religion is giving way to spirituality* (Oxford, Blackwell, 2005)

Paul Heelas and Linda Woodhead, 'Homeless minds today?' in Linda

Woodhead (ed.), *Peter Berger and the Study of Religion* (London, Routledge, 2002)

William D. Hendricks, *Exit Interviews* (Chicago, Moody Press, 1993)

Richard Higginson, *Transforming Leadership* (London, SPCK, 1996)

Alan Hirsch, *The Forgotten Ways* (Grand Rapids, Brazos Press, 2006)

John H. Holland, *Emergence: From Chaos to Order* (Oxford, Oxford University Press, 2000)

John Inge, *A Christian Theology of Place* (Aldershot, Ashgate, 2003)

Eric O. Jacobsen, *Sidewalks in the Kingdom: New Urbanism and the Christian Faith* (Grand Rapids MI, Brazos Press, 2003)

Alan Jamieson, *A Churchless Faith* (London, SPCK, 2002)

Alan Jamieson, Jenny McIntosh and Adrienne Thompson, *Church Leavers* (London, SPCK, 2006)

Peter Jarvis, *Adult and Continuing Education: Theory and Practice* (London, Routledge, 1995)

Philip Jenkins, *The Next Christendom*, 2nd edn (New York, Oxford University Press, 2007)

Richard A. Jensen, *Thinking in Story: Preaching in a Post-Literate Age* (Lima OH, CSS Publishing Co, 1993)

Steven Johnson, *Emergence: The connected lives of ants, brains, cities, and software* (New York, Penguin, 2001)

Rhawn Joseph (ed.), *Neurotheology: Brain, Science, Spirituality, Religious Experience* (San Jose CA, San Jose University Press, 2003)

Gordon Lynch, *Understanding Theology and Popular Culture* (Oxford, Blackwell, 2005)

Michel Maffesoli, *The Time of Tribes: Decline of Individualism in Mass Society* (Thousand Oaks CA, Sage, 1995)

David Martin, *On Secularization: Towards a revised general theory* (Aldershot, Ashgate, 2005).

Abraham Maslow, *Toward a Psychology of Being*, 2nd edn (New York, Van Nostrand Reinhold, 1968)

E. Mazur and K. McCarthy, *God in the Details: American Religion in Popular Culture* (New York, Routledge, 2001)

M. Rex Miller, *The Millennium Matrix. Reclaiming the Past, Reframing the Future of the Church* (San Francisco, Jossey-Bass, 2004)

Stuart Murray, *Post-Christendom* (Carlisle, Paternoster Press, 2004)

Stuart Murray, *Church after Christendom* (Carlisle, Paternoster Press 2005)

Stuart Murray, *Changing Mission: Learning from Newer Churches* (London, CTBI, 2006)

Andrew Newberg and Eugene D'Aquili, *Why God won't go away: Brain science and the biology of belief* (New York, Ballantine, 2002)

Lesslie Newbigin, *The Gospel in a Pluralist Society* (Grand Rapids MI, Eerdmans, 1992)

Thomas C. Oden, *After Modernity – What?* (Grand Rapids MI, Eerdmans, 1990)

Walter Ong, *Orality and Literacy*, 2nd edn (New York, Routledge, 2002)

Conrad Oswalt, *Secular Steeples* (Harrisburg PA, Trinity Press International, 2003)

Richard Pascale, Mark Millemann and Linda Gioja, *Surfing the Edge of Chaos* (New York, Random House, 2001)

John E. Paver, *Theological Reflection and Education for Ministry* (Aldershot, Ashgate, 2006)

Richard V. Peace, *Conversion in the New Testament* (Grand Rapids MI, Eerdmans, 1999)

Myron B. Penner, *Christianity and the Postmodern Turn* (Grand Rapids MI, Brazos Press, 2005)

Martyn Percy, *Engaging with Contemporary Culture* (Aldershot, Ashgate, 2005)

B. Joseph Pine and James H. Gilmore, *The Experience Economy* (Boston MA, Harvard Business School, 1999)

Daniel Pink, *A Whole New Mind* (New York, Riverhead Books, 2006)

Christine D. Pohl, *Making Room: Recovering Hospitality as a Christian Tradition* (Grand Rapids MI, Eerdmans, 1999)

Robert D. Putnam, *Bowling Alone: The collapse and revival of American community* (New York, Simon & Schuster, 2000)

Paul H. Ray and Sherry Ruth Anderson, *The Cultural Creatives* (New York, Three Rivers Press, 2000)

Anne Richards, *Sense Making Faith* (London, CTBI, 2007)

Philip J. Richter and Leslie J. Francis, *Gone but not Forgotten* (London, Darton, Longman & Todd, 1998)

Michael Riddell, Mark Pierson and Cathy Kirkpatrick, *The Prodigal Project: Journeying into the emerging church* (London, SPCK, 2000)

George Ritzer, *The McDonaldization of Society* (Thousand Oaks CA, Pine Forge Press, 1993)

George Ritzer (ed.), *McDonaldization: The Reader*, 2nd edn (Thousand Oaks CA, Pine Forge Press, 2006)

Wade Clark Roof, *Spiritual Marketplace* (Princeton NJ, Princeton University Press, 1999)

Richard Rohr, *Simplicity: The art of living* (New York, Crossroad, 1991)

Alan J. Roxburgh and Fred Romanuk, *The Missional Leader* (San Francisco, Jossey-Bass, 2006)

Tex Sample, *Ministry in an Oral Culture* (Louisville KY, Westminster John Knox Press, 1994)

Ziauddin Sardar, *Postmodernism and the Other* (London, Pluto Press, 1998)

Kenneth Schuman and Ronald Paxton, *The Michelangelo Method* (New York, McGraw-Hill, 2007)

John Shore, *Penguins, Pain and the Whole Shebang* (New York, Seabury Books, 2005)

David Smith, *Mission after Christendom* (London, Darton, Longman & Todd, 2003)

Ian Stackhouse, *Gospel Driven Church* (Carlisle, Paternoster Press, 2004)

Brian Stone, *Evangelism after Christendom* (Grand Rapids MI, Brazos Press, 2007)

Barry Taylor, *Entertainment Theology: New-edge spirituality in a digital democracy* (Grand Rapids MI, Baker Academic, 2008)

Steve Taylor, *The Out of Bounds Church* (Grand Rapids MI: Zondervan 2005)

F. M. L. Thomson, *The Rise of Suburbia* (Leicester, Leicester University Press, 1982)

Kevin Treston, *Creative Christian Leadership* (Mystic CT, Twenty-Third Publications, 2000)

Jean M. Twenge, *Generation Me* (New York, Free Press, 2006)

Kevin J. Vanhoozer, Charles A. Anderson, and Michael J. Sleasman, *Everyday Theology* (Grand Rapids MI, Baker Academic, 2007)

Andrew Walker and Luke Bretherton, *Remembering our Future* (London, Paternoster Press, 2007)

Pete Ward, *Liquid Church* (Peabody MA, Hendrickson, 2002)

Ethan Watters, *Urban Tribes* (New York, Bloomsbury, 2003)

Robert E. Webber, *Ancient-Future Faith* (Grand Rapids MI, Baker Academic, 1999)

Robert E. Webber, *Ancient-Future Evangelism* (Grand Rapids MI, Baker Academic, 2003)

Robert E. Webber, *Ancient-Future Time* (Grand Rapids MI, Baker Academic, 2004)

John H. Westerhoff III, *Will our Children have Faith?*, 2nd edn (Harrisburg, PA, Morehouse, 2000)

Peter C. Whybrow, *American Mania. When more is not enough* (New York, Norton, 2005)

Philip B. Wilson, *Being Single in the Church Today: Insights from History and Personal Stories* (Harrisburg PA, Morehouse, 2005)

Walter Wink, *Transforming Bible Study*, 2nd edn (Nashville TN, Abingdon, 1990)

INDEX

Note: where reference is made to endnotes, and in cases where more than one sequence of notes appears on the same page, they are distinguished by the addition of a or b following the note number.

agriculture, agricultural 17–18, 20, 31, 34–5, 44, 57, 83–4
alienation *see* loneliness
Alpha course 81, 90, 116
Amish 17, 53
Anderson, Ray S. 51–2, 148 n.57
Anderson, Sherry Ruth 135, 137, 138, 140, 154 n.35
arts *see* creativity
Astley, Jeff 43, 122, 133, 137
atheism, atheist *see* secular
Atkinson, David ix

Barna, George 144 n.10
Barth, Karl 50, 142
Batey, Richard A. 147 n.24
Bauckham, Richard J. 148 n.47
Baylor University 144 n.11, 150 n.20
Berger, Birgitte 33
Berger, Peter 33, 34, 38–9, 40, 46
Berryman, Jerome 137
Bewes, Richard 115
blogs, blogging *see* computers, computing
Bolger, Ryan 49
Borg, Marcus 147 n.39
Bosch, David J. 148 n.48
Bretherton, Luke 151 n.22, 152 n.19
Brewin, Kester 47–8

Brierley, Peter 144 n.8, 150 n.12, 151 n.1
Brookes, Andrew 152 n.18
Brown, Callum 140
Brown, Dan 14, 116
Browning, Don S. 153 n.15
Buechner, Carl W. 44
Burridge, Richard A. 148 n.47
Buttrick, David 152 n.15

Calvin, John 6
Cambridge, Cambridgeshire 15, 33
Carr, C. M. H. 146 n.13
Carrette, Jeremy 149 n.10
Carson, D. A. 48
Cartesian *see* Descartes
Cartledge, Mark 153 n.11
Chicago (musical) 57
Christ, Christology 49–52, 56, 86, 114, 121
Christendom 6, 23–5, 51, 53, 59, 89, 91, 95, 105, 107, 110, 112
Church, churches:
 American 4–5, 93, 94
 Anglican 3–4, 24, 47, 51, 77, 139
 Baptist 19, 51
 Canadian 5
 charismatic 83–5, 84–5, 87, 127, 150 n.22
 Congregational 19, 51

decline of vii, 3–5, 46, 93
denominations 3–4, 43, 45–6, 52, 63–4, 83–4, 87, 94–5, 98, 107, 122, 126 emerging 47–58, 85, 115–16, 147 n.39
    Fresh Expressions of 47–8
    leavers 3, 42–4, 45, 99–101, 115
    Methodist 4, 19, 47, 51
    mission statements of 59
    Presbyterian 106
    Reformed 4
    Roman Catholic 51, 54, 60, 63, 83, 94, 149 n.3
    Scottish 59–62, 63, 124
    statistics 3–5, 75–6, 93, 149 n.11
    World Council of 23–4
cities, city living 34, 37, 38–40, 46, 57
    regeneration of 60–1
community, change in 31–4
    new forms of 38–40
    and mission 40–58
computers, computing 10, 12, 17, 19, 31–2, 34–5, 110
Constantine 5, 51
consumerism 6, 20, 43–4
Cottrell, Stephen 40, 59
Coupland, Douglas 29–30, 55
Cox, Harvey 144 n.22
creativity vii, 49, 56–7, 60–4, 113–14, 135–41
Cresswell, Jamie 144 n.2
Croft, Steven 148 n.52
cuddle party 33
culture, cultural change, vii, 8–23, 29, 31–4, 125–8, 141
    and church 2–7, 40–58, 67–8, 82–6, 93–6, 101–4
    and club scene 27–8, 69, 71
    and demographics 32–3, 34
    and values 118–20
Cupitt, Don 133

Davies, John ix
Da Vinci Code (novel) 14, 116

Dawes, Gregory W. 148 n.47
Dawkins, Richard 77, 153 n.1
Descartes, René 7, 112, 125, 132
Detroit 80
Didache 89

ecclesiology 51–2, 83–4, 121
Edinburgh 88, 124
Edson, Ben 49
education 19, 26, 73–4, 118–120
    theological 2–3, 64, 74, 95–6, 116–17, 132–42
Einstein, Albert 111, 125, 137
emergence 39–40
Enlightenment, European 7–8, 23; see also modernity
Epistle to Diognetus 89
Erikson, Erik 69
eschatology 16, 27, 52, 56
Eucharist 54
evangelical, evangelicalism 20, 64, 110, 114–15, 139
    post- 48

faith, as lifestyle 6–7, 14–15, 65, 78–9, 82–6, 88–9, 115–16, 131
    as belief 45, 65, 78, 81, 90–1, 118, 123–4
    development of 89–92
family 17–20, 31–3, 36–7, 38, 68–9, 72
farming see agriculture
fear 15–16, 26, 37, 53, 62, 108; see also eschatology
Fearnley-Whittingstall, Hugh 7
Fielding, Helen 146 n.5
Fishman, Robert 146 n.14
Fleming Drane, O. M. ix, 146 n.3, 147 n.29, 149 n.4, 5
Florence 113–14
Florida, Richard 56, 66
Fowler, James 89
Francis, Leslie J. 147 n.27
Frost, Michael 1

Fuller Seminary 1, 26, 97, 137–8
Fung, Raymond 23–4, 151 n.29

Gallagher, R. 20
Gandalf 104
generations see people groups
Gibbs, Eddie 49
Gilmore, James H. 24, 102–3
Gioja, Linda 146 n.18
Glasgow 60–4, 99, 124
Gledhill, Ruth 77
Globalization 25, 30, 31, 127–8
   and church 4, 13, 67, 126–8
Gospels (New Testament) see Jesus
Gutiérrez, Gustavo 126

Harrison, Kate 146 n.7
Hawkins, Greg 152 n.11
Hay, David 14, 150 n.17
Hayden, Dolores 146 n.14
health, healthcare 15, 31, 70, 73–4,
   123, 128
hedonism, hedonists 27, 65, 70–1, 72,
   75, 81–2, 88
Heelas, Paul 46–7, 52
Hendricks, William D. 147 n.27
Higginson, Richard 152 n.9
Hippolytus 89
Hirsch, Alan 1
Hitchens, Christopher 153 n.1
Holland, John H. 146 n.18
Hollywood 110
Holy Spirit 52, 66, 107
homeless 33, 34, 46–7, 70, 80–1
hope see eschatology
hospitality see community: and
   mission
Hunt, Kate 14
Hunt, Stephen J. 144 n.23

identity, personal 66–78, 80; see also
   individualism, loneliness
individualism 20, 32–4, 36–7, 40, 74,
   114; see also loneliness

industry, industrialists, industrial
   revolution 17, 18–19, 20, 21, 31–2,
   34–5, 44, 83–4
information see computers,
   computing
internet see computers, computing
intuition 65–6; see also creativity
Islam 7, 25

Jacobsen, Eric O. 146 n.11
Jacobsen, Marion Leach 41
Jamieson, Alan 100, 144 n.7
Jarvis, Peter 154 n.19
Jenkins, Philip 126
Jesus 41, 44, 49–50, 52, 53, 54, 55,
   57, 62–3, 77, 86, 101, 105, 106,
   113, 114, 116, 117, 121, 122, 137,
   140
Johnson, Steven 146 n.18
Jones, Bridget 32–3, 71
Joseph, Rhawn 150 n.17

Kellner, Hansfried 33
Kendal 14, 46–7
King, Martin Luther Jr. 104
King, Richard 149 n.10
Kirkpatrick, Cathy 42
Kreider, Alan 152 n.19

Lancaster, University of 46
leadership 13, 56, 93–117
Lewis, C. S. 90–1
life, lifestyle 5–7, 11, 29–31
   and cities 37–40
   and mission 65, 78–9, 80–1, 85,
      88–92, 115–16
   and suburbs 34–7
   and work 17–23
Lillie, William 136–7
Lings, George 13
Lischer, Richard 131
liturgy, liturgical see worship
loneliness 32–3, 36–7, 38, 39–40, 45,
   49, 57, 71, 74–5

and church 41–4, 46
  see also individualism
Luther, Martin 86
Lynch, Gordon 144 n.19
Lyotard, François 112

Macdonald, Fergus 88
Maclaine, Shirley 14, 82
McCullough, Leigh 149 n.6
McDonaldization, 1–2, 5–7, 44–5, 57,
    64–5, 70, 106, 115, 134, 141, 144
    n.12
McGavran, Donald 152 n.10
McIntosh, Jenny 152 n.3
McLaren, Brian 48
Maffesoli, Michael 146 n.16
Manchester 49
Marriage 33, 68–9
Martin, David 145 n.34
Marx, Groucho ix
Maslow, Abraham 80
Mayland, Jean 139
Michelangelo 113–14
migration 22, 30–1, 34–5
Millemann, Mark 146 n.18
Mission Theological Advisory
    Group ix
modernity 7, 10, 16, 25, 33, 111
Moses 120
Murray, Stuart 91
Muslim *see* Islam

narrative *see* stories
Newberg, Andrew 150 n.17
Newbigin, Lesslie 91, 136
New England 18

Oden, Thomas 25
Ong, Walter 72

Parkes, Sharon Daloz 57–8
Parkinson, Cally 152 n.11
Pascale, Richard 146 n.18
Paul, Pamela 146 n.7

Paxton, Ronald 152 n.14
Pennsylvania 17
Pentecost, festival of 42, 61–4
    Pentecostal, Pentecostalism 13,
        126–7, 150 n.22
    see also church: charismatic
people groups 64–78, 79, 80–2
    children 16, 99
    teenagers 15–16
    young adults 26–7, 67, 100
    see also hedonist, tradition,
        spiritual
Percy, Martyn 9, 63, 128–9, 131, 139,
    144 n.20
Philo 120–1
Pierson, Mark 42
Pine, B. Joseph 21, 102–3
Pink, Daniel H. viii, 16–17, 21–2, 31,
    56, 135
Plymouth Brethren 54
Pohl, Christine D. 54–5
politics, politicians 15, 27, 34, 70, 101,
    119
post-modern, post-modernity 8–10,
    16, 64, 71, 85, 110, 128; *see also*
    culture
Potter, Harry 104
Pritchard, G. A. 152 n.11
psychology 26, 33, 67, 89, 114, 123
Putnam, Robert D. 146 n.21

Ray, Paul 135, 137, 138, 140, 154 n.35
Rees, Martin 15
Reformation, Reformers 6, 51
religion, religious organizations 19,
    21, 31, 34, 40–1, 50, 73, 81, 104,
    127–8
    New Religious Movements 13
Richards, Anne 144, n.4a
Richter, Philip J. 147 n.27
Riddell, Michael 42
Ritzer, George 1, 14, 148 n.49
Rohr, Richard 89
Romanuk, Fred 16, 113, 146 n.15

Roxburgh, Alan J. 16, 113, 146 n.15
rural *see* agriculture

Saliba, John A. 144 n.23
Santa Barbara 81
Sardar, Ziauddin 144 n.14
Schleiermacher, Friedrich 123–4
Schuman, Kenneth 152 n.14
Scientology 13
Scotland, Scottish 18, 24, 42, 59–60, 119, 124
secular, secularization, secularist 9, 14, 20–1, 53, 75–7, 81–2, 118–19
Shakers 53
Shermer, Michael 76
Shore, John 27, 41–2
singleness 32–3, 94
social sciences, sociology 1, 20, 67, 123, 144 n.23
Soldz, Stephen 149 n.6
space, private 36–7
    third 56–7
Spiderman 104
spiritual, spirituality: 13–15, 20–1, 25–6, 34, 45–6, 65, 70, 72–3, 75, 76–7, 78–82, 85, 88–9, 104, 109, 114, 119, 127, 135; *see also* faith
Stackhouse, Ian 151 n.31
Starbucks 56–7
Stirling 42, 60
stories, storytelling viii, 39, 111–14, 135
suburbs, suburbia 34–7, 40, 44, 46, 57

television 12, 19, 29
Teresa, Mother 104

Thompson, Adrienne 152 n.3
Thomson, F. M. L. 146 n.13
Tomlinson, Dave 147 n.41
tradition, traditionalist 71–2, 73, 81, 84
Treston, Kevin 152 n.8
Turner, Victor 49
Twenge, Jean M. 26, 145 n.32, 146 n.4

Unification church 13
United Nations 34
urban tribes 38–40, 54, 56–7, 135; *see also* cities

Von Stradonitz, F. K. 65–6

Walker, Andrew 151 n.22, 152 n.19
Watters, Ethan 38–9, 56
Webber, Robert 55
Westerhoff, John H. 89
Whitehead, J. D. 154 n.17
Williams, Rowan 48
Willow Creek 152 n.11
Wilson, Bryan 144 n.23
Wilson, Philip B. 151 n.2
Windsor 27
Wink, Walter 137
Winston, Robert 123
Woodhead, Linda 46–7, 52
worldviews 7–11, 22–6, 125–8; *see also* culture
worldwide web *see* computers, computing
work *see* lifestyle
worship 18, 19, 20, 44, 45, 62–3, 83–4, 87, 99, 109, 114–15, 137

Bible References

Old Testament

Genesis 1:1–2:4a   vii
Genesis 1:27   11, 56, 132
1 Samuel 17:38–40   142
Psalms, book of   88

New Testament

Matthew 7:24–7   114
Mark 3:35   41
Mark 9:40   54
Mark 12:28–34   137
Luke 7:31–4   54
Luke 10:1–12   44, 62
Luke 14:15–24   54

John 1:14   121
John 14:26   66
Acts 2:1–42   61
Romans, letter to   86
Romans 12:2   148 n.53
Romans 8:26   24
1 Corinthians 12:1–31   105
Galatians 5:22–3   43
Ephesians 2:19–22   114
Ephesians 4:11   95
Colossians 2:6–7   114
James 4:4   148 n.53
1 Peter 2:4–5   114
1 John 1   121